SURPRISED by FAITH

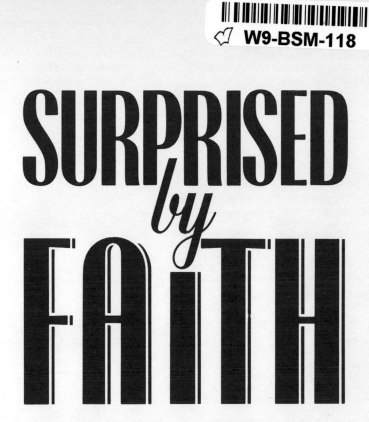

*A Scientist Shares His Personal,
Life-Changing Discoveries About God,
The Bible, And Personal Fulfillment*

Dr. Don Bierle

This Billy Graham Evangelistic Association
special edition is published with permission
from Emerald Books.

Emerald
Books

P.O. Box 635
Lynnwood, Washington 98046

Surprised by Faith

ISBN 0-913367-90-7

Published by Emerald Books
P.O. Box 635
Lynnwood, WA 98046

CONTENTS

ACKNOWLEDGMENTS

This book has been in preparation for many years. Not the manuscript, per se, but the substance has been tested in thousands of lives over the past two decades. I am grateful to the students in my college classes whose feedback has been insightful. But it is to the thousands who have attended the H.I.S. Ministries home series, *The Faith Study*, that I dedicate this book. They have questioned, encouraged, dialogued, stimulated, rejoiced, rejected, wept, debated, inspired, and otherwise kept my feet on the ground. They are the "flesh and blood" of this book, and my joy.

Special thanks go to Joel Allen, David Lundstrom, and Jake Barnett for reading the manuscript and giving many helpful suggestions. To Jake, especially, I am grateful for his toughness, and for keeping me honest and consistent. I also thank my friend, Nathan Unseth, for his expertise in seeing the manuscript through to publication.

I am particularly appreciative of the time and encouragement to write that has been given me by the Board of Directors of H.I.S. Ministries. They are always there when I need them, my faithful friends.

Finally, I owe much to God's special gift to me, my wife Vernee. She was an early catalyst in my faith journey, and continues to give unselfishly as we share life and ministry together. In a real sense, she is the unsung coauthor of this book.

PREFACE

It seems I have always been in school. Twenty-three years of my life have been spent in formal education from the elementary level through my doctorate. For another twenty-three years I have been on the other side of the classroom desk as a college administrator and professor. The intellectual stimulation of the academic environment has undoubtedly shaped the development of my thought. I have always viewed books as wonderfully positive, treasures to explore. Even in the one-room rural school where I attended for grades 1-8, I remember reading nearly every book our teacher could check out of the town library. Even today I have little sales resistance to the delectable fare served up by publishers' flyers and catalogs that cross my desk.

It also seems I have always thought about God. Growing up in a family that took seriously its Christian heritage, I had considerable exposure to religious instruction. But beyond that, in my private thoughts, I recall often walking along the creek that went through our farm, and wondering "why" about everything from droughts to the death of my pet dog. A hunger for ultimate answers goes back as far as I can remember. My quest for meaning was evident even to the old German minister of our church, and prompted his special visit when I was fourteen to encourage my parents to have me prepare for the Christian ministry. At the time, and during the subsequent few years, I did not see "the church" as a source for answers. The field of science had caught my fascination. It satisfied, for a time and to some degree, my inquisitiveness about the world and life.

When you add the attribute of competitiveness to the two ingredients of extensive education and hunger for ultimate answers, you have the formula for an intense search for purpose. This is the background for much of the autobiographical material included in this book. Most of my struggles came during my college and early graduate education. At that time I turned from what I perceived as the restrictive intellectual climate of traditional religion. In its place I found the liberating attitudes of science which I thought held out promise for the fulfillment I was seeking. During this time I mentally either discarded or challenged much of traditional Christian teaching about the Bible, creation, Jesus Christ and salvation. I was asking "why," and could not find the answers. At times I felt there must be something wrong with me since so many said they "believed" without needing answers.

I now realize there was nothing wrong with my need for answers, and that I was not alone. I was also fortunate. At the height of my search I became acquainted with people who had found answers. For them, intellect was not the enemy of faith. My encounter with them established a reasonable foundation for faith that has reset the direction of my life. Fulfillment had at last come to me.

Many years have passed since then. My understanding of the evidence and reasons in support of the Christian faith has increased significantly. During the last fifteen years I have presented what I have learned to groups of interested people meeting in private homes. More than 10,000 have now attended, many who have been quite skeptical, including agnostics and atheists. My goal has been to create a respectful and non-threatening intellectual environment to investigate faith, including the use of logic and scientific evidence. The most frequent comment that I continue to hear from believer and skeptic alike is, "I have never heard of this before! I didn't know there were reasons."

I am writing this book for those who have not been as fortunate as I was to find answers. My heart goes out to everyone who cares for truth and the meaning of life but thinks that the Christian faith is intellectually unacceptable. I am also concerned for those who have felt frustrated with the inability to communicate the reasons for their faith in terms that make sense to outsiders. In either case, I believe there is help here.

In the writing of the book I have attempted to integrate two distinct elements:

(1) a recounting of my personal intellectual struggles and experiences, and

(2) subsequent developments in my understanding through research and mature reflection. I have tried to make the distinction clear throughout. For example, most of the diagrams in the text were added later to clarify some aspect of my earlier struggle. Likewise, the insight gained from some of the biblical stories and illustrations came only after later study and reflection. My purpose in adding both to the book is to give the reader a more complete perspective about faith.

The apostle Peter commanded that we should "Always be prepared to give an answer to everyone who asks you to give the reason for the hope that you have. But do this with gentleness and respect..." That's what I have tried to do. I hope it will help some to find the path to faith.

"I used my wisdom to test all of this. I was determined to be wise, but it was beyond me. How can anyone discover what life means? It is too deep for us, too hard to understand. But I devoted myself to knowledge and study; I was determined to find wisdom and the answers to my questions..."
Ecclesiastes 7:23-25 (paraphrase)

ONE
WHAT AM I HERE FOR?

The Crisis Of
Purpose And Meaning

"Death is the ultimate statistic. One out of one die."
  George Bernard Shaw, dramatist

"He's a real nowhere man
Sitting in his nowhere land
Making all his nowhere plans for nobody.

Doesn't have a point of view,
Knows not where he's going to—
Isn't he a bit like me and you?
  John Lennon and Paul McCartney, the Beatles

*S*ome might question my right to teach about faith because I have not always thought kindly of it. As an athlete at a
midwestern college, I would enjoy the occasional fun we jocks
had mocking the religious types on campus. Later, as a biology
graduate student, I cherished the day that a certain religious
magazine arrived in another student's office. That occasion became a special time for us scientists in several disciplines to
gather for an exposure of the naivity of people who wrote in
such publications.

Personal Caricatures of Faith

During my undergraduate and graduate studies in the natural sciences, I was cynical about faith and religious people. I
viewed faith as anti-intellectual, an excuse for a lack of hard

knowledge. Science dealt with objective truth in the real world. Religious faith was not truth; it was whatever a person believed. The strongest faith was that which a believer held on to without real evidence, indeed, in spite of evidence to the contrary!

Furthermore, I caricatured faith as an emotion. It was a kind of security blanket for the less informed and insecure. These people used religion as a drug for its emotional effect, both to stimulate and to calm. But I suspected that it was an illusion. In reality, there was no substance there.

It was my third caricature that revealed the most about me. I felt that faith was a crutch for weak people. My science associates agreed. It was okay for those who were not able to handle life, but as for me, "I was doing fine without it, thank you!"

But this view was not entirely coherent. It was unsatisfying in my struggle with the significant issues of life. I, like others, struggled with questions and fears concerning death, feelings of personal guilt, and an awareness of an ultimate lack of meaning. Clark Pinnock, a contemporary theologian, writes what I felt at that time:

> We are experiencing...a loss of meaning in our time... According to humanism, for example, a man or a woman comes into the world devoid of any inherent worth, meaning or direction, entirely on their own. There is no larger purposive order in which their lives participate. There is no significance or value for them which they do not create for themselves. They are driven logically to sympathize with Macbeth: 'Life is a tale, told by an idiot, full of sound and fury, signifying nothing.'[1]

Why was I on planet earth? What significance and value did my life have? The Russian novelist, Tolstoy, put it this way: "What is life for? To die? To kill myself at once? No, I am afraid. To wait for death till it comes? I fear that even more. Then I must live. But what for? In order to die? And I could not escape from that circle."[2] It was questions like these that led me to a reexamination of the nature of faith. I came to the realization that my perspective was really a caricature — a cartoon distortion of faith, not the real thing.

"The question of the meaning and worth of life never becomes more urgent or more agonizing than when we see the final breath leave a body which a moment before was living."
Carl Jung, psychologist.

The Crisis of Purpose and Meaning without Faith

Identifying the Problem: A Finite Orphan

Perhaps an illustration would help at this point. Imagine with me that the entire known universe has vanished. It is entirely gone. We, too, no longer exist. Now let us imagine that some soil appears in this vacuum. To indicate its finiteness, we will put it inside a triangle. What is its purpose? Every response to that question will assume the existence of something else. For example, it is for growing plants, or a foundation for trees or buildings. But if soil is truly the *only* thing that exists, it has no reason to be.

Figure 1.

To solve the soil's problem, grass suddenly appears with soil in our imaginary universe. The soil now has a purpose — to grow grass. But what of the grass? In a universe consisting of only dirt and grass, what is the purpose for grass? Most will suggest that it is for food or beauty or to enjoy its softness under foot. But nothing exists that eats or looks or can enjoy a walk in its thickness. The grass stands alone with the soil.[3]

Figure 2.

Alternatively, grass would find purpose within the context of a universe that includes cows. The grass now exists so that cows can live. But what shall we say for the cows' purpose? To fertilize the grass? To produce milk? But, for what or whom? In a finite world, individual cows may die in order to make room for more cows. However, this suggests that the only purpose of the death of purposeless cows is to make room for more purposeless cows. This is not a satisfying answer and leaves us right where we started. What is the purpose?

Figure 3.

Our problem to this point has been that no reasoning creatures are present. Only intelligent life can make sense out of this new planet. Dirt, grass and cows could not recognize purpose. What is needed is a reasoning and logical being—a being that can think and experience esthetic values. We need a race of beings like humankind. With humankind now in place it is all complete. The soil exists so the grass can grow. The grass finds purpose in providing for the cow. And the soil, grass, and cows are there so that humankind can live with meaning and purpose.

But what is that purpose? Why *do* people exist on this new planet? In his finite condition the best that he can answer is to "dig in the dirt", "mow the grass" and "milk the cow"! Is there nothing more? This is Tolstoy's dilemma: "What is life for? To die?"

"Life is just a dirty trick, a short journey from nothingness to nothingness."

Ernest Hemingway, American novelist.

This has been a basic question in philosophy for the past 3000 years, and as yet is still unanswered. In fact, most modern philosophy's answer is to say, "I give up".

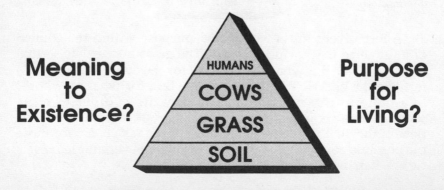

The finite triangle is left entirely alone in space. There is nothing else. All the beings are cosmic orphans. Did we create a different world from our own? No! This is our present world of inanimate matter (soil), botanical and zoological organisms, and man. Pinnock points out the problem well:

> Does everyone in fact feel this drive toward meaning...How is it that there are those who do not seem to ask this question? Many...have uncomplicated assumptions about meaning and take a great deal for granted. If life has been good to them, they probably have some personal goals—in their job or marriage—which give them enough satisfaction that the question of deeper meaning seems a bit remote. Unfortunately, however, the realities of life have a way of ganging up on a person with shallow assumptions. Something almost always comes along to shatter the dream and raise the issue of meaning for them...which may come in the form of illness or inflation or the loss of a loved one. There are all manner of threats to the meaning of our lives both internal and external which can conspire to destroy it if it is inadequately grounded.[4]

Illustrating the Problem: A Terminal Disease

This lack of a higher purpose and meaning was illustrated to me recently in a conversation with a friend at a class reunion. When I asked him, "What are you doing now?", he responded at some length but in essence said, "I work." I then asked why he was in that type of work and he responded, "Because it pays well." "But why do you need so much money?" I asked. "To live!" he said as he recounted his house and car payments, educational costs, and recreational needs. The acid test came with the question, "But why do you live?" After a blank stare he quipped, "To work". He was caught in the same purposeless cycle that many are:

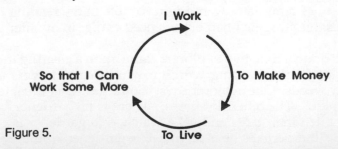

Figure 5.

It has never dawned on many that some morning they will not show up for work!

"It's not that I'm afraid to die, I just don't want to be there when it happens..."
Woody Allen, Film director and comedian

If they could look back upon their life they would likely ask, "What was that about anyway?" As a high school senior and college student, I recall struggling with a decision about vocational choice. I intuitively felt that I wanted my life to count for something. Most of the advice I got was based on economics, where I could make a good living. But I felt that life must ultimately have more value than anticipating a big paycheck. Otherwise, in terms of the triangle illustration, I was no better off than the dirt, the grass and the cow. At that time in my young life, I did not know the way out of this dilemma.

Constructing a Solution: The "God Hypothesis"

It seemed that the only people I knew back then who were not bothered by this dilemma were religious ones. Their response was, "Don, God is the answer." But when I asked how they knew there was a God, they would respond that I just needed to believe in Him without questioning. This would only reinforce my view that people of faith and religion were really anti-intellectual. There were no reasons. Reason had nothing to do with faith.

Wishful Thinking or Objective Reality?

Recently I came across a modern parable in my reading that illustrates this struggle I had experienced earlier in my life:

Once upon a time two explorers came upon a clearing in the jungle. In the clearing were growing many flowers and many weeds. One explorer says, "Some gardener must tend this plot." The other disagrees, "There is no gardener." So they pitch their tents and set a watch. No gardener is ever seen. "But perhaps he is an invisible gardener." So they set up a barbed wire fence. They electrify it. They patrol with bloodhounds... But no shrieks ever suggest that some intruder has received a shock. No movements of the wire ever betray an invisible climber. The bloodhounds never give cry. Yet still the believer is not convinced. "But there is a gardener, invisible, insensible to electric shocks, a gardener who comes secretly to look after the garden which he loves." At last the skeptic despairs, "But what remains of your original assertion? Just how does what you call an invisible, intangible, eternally elusive gardener differ from an imaginary gardener or even from no gardener at all?[5]

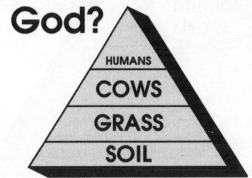

Figure 6.

If the soil, grass, cows and people are not just finite orphans floating through an otherwise empty universe, and if they are going to have a higher purpose than annihilation at death, then a God needs to exist. But just to wish for Him, does not make Him exist. How could someone ever know the difference between a God who is really there and one created by man's wishful thinking?

"In the form in which men have posed it, the Riddle of the Universe requires a theological answer. Suffering and enjoying, men want to know why they enjoy and to what end they suffer. They see good things and evil things, beautiful things and ugly, and they want to find a reason—a final and absolute reason—why these things should be as they are."

Aldous Huxley, English author

A Testable Strategy

The answer to me was simple. If there is a real God, the only way I could know for certain was for Him to come to where He could be seen, heard and touched. I wanted to see Him in real history, but I couldn't imagine that actually happening. Subsequently, I have come to realize that this line of thinking was appropriate. It was the basis for focusing on a very practical theological test. I now see it in terms of the triangle illustration: Is it conceivable that the infinite God might come into the finite world of soil, grass, cows and humans?

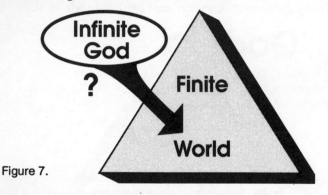

Figure 7.

"If God does not exist...man is in consequence forlorn, for he cannot find anything to depend upon, either within or outside himself."

Jean Paul Sartre, French existentialist philosopher

Two Essential Characteristics of God

Analysis during the years since my original struggle has given me additional insights. The writings of the late Dr. Francis Schaeffer, philosopher and theologian, have been particularly helpful. He argues that a God who would be adequate to solve the problem of purpose and meaning, and explain man's personal nature, would have to possess certain characteristics. In particular, two are critical. [6]

1. *God must be infinite.* An infinite God is one who by definition is complete and entirely perfect, lacking nothing. He must exist outside the finite triangle or I could rightly ask, "What is

God's purpose?" Being infinite makes such a question of God meaningless. If purpose were not inherent in His being, He would not be infinite. Likewise, if God were not infinite, He would be of no help in solving the problem of purpose and meaning of the finite, including myself. Furthermore, He would be incapable of creating the triangle and placing it in space in the first place.

2. *God must be personal.* Personal beings communicate and are capable of love. They build relationships. They do not talk to the wind or fire. They do not have a relationship with a radar beam. Electricity cannot reciprocate my affection.

Likewise, the "Force" will never suffice for God. Only a personal being capable of communication and love would satisfy my desire for a relationship with Him. A 'universal spirit' concept of God, while putting Him everywhere, actually puts God nowhere in particular. Only a God who was "someone" rather than "something" could possibly show up in the triangle and be seen, heard and touched.

World Religions on Trial

People all over the world, which is our finite triangle, claim to know there is a God. But they do not agree at all on what He is like. With a broad brush let's classify all the religions according to their views on the two essential characteristics of God identified above. They fall into three basic categories.

Eastern Thought. Religions like Buddhism and Hinduism maintain that God is indeed infinite. God is the source and sustainer of all that exists. But God is not a personal being. Instead, all is God and God is all. There is no one there — no emotion, no love, no communication. There is no one to get to know. God is an impersonal, universal spirit, not someone to see, hear or touch. He is infinite, yet impersonal, like the wind.

Furthermore, an impersonal God does not provide for a grounding in moral questions of good and evil. In Hinduism, there is both a good and a bad force. Nothing is ultimately right or wrong.

"When the ship is going down, what difference does it make whether one stands on deck and salutes or plays a last game of poker?"

Jean Paul Sartre, *No Exit.*

Also, Hinduism doesn't answer the question, "How can I be personal? Where does self-awareness, self-consciousness, personality come from?" The Hindu would answer, "To know God as impersonal requires that we deny our personality." Chanting "Om" is a pursuit of mindlessness, destructive to personality, in order to know God.

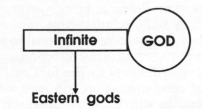

Figure 8.

Western Thought. The Greeks and Nordic peoples had a different idea. Anyone who has read the mythologies knows that their gods are very personal and knowable beings. They have clear personalities. The problem is that they have more troubles than we do. They are not infinite. They fight, lust and otherwise demonstrate that they are inadequate in themselves. They cannot solve our need to find ultimate purpose and meaning.

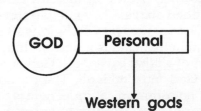

Figure 9.

Three Exceptions. What are we to do? The East has religions that claim an infinite God exists, but is not personal. I have to believe such a God exists but I have no way to know such a God in the finite triangle in which I live.

The West has religions that claim personal gods that are knowable but inadequate. The Western gods are not infinite and cannot offer an answer to ultimate purpose and meaning.

There are, however, three religions that claim a God that is both infinite *and* personal. Judaism, Christianity, and Islam teach that God is both infinite Creator and a personal being that can be known.

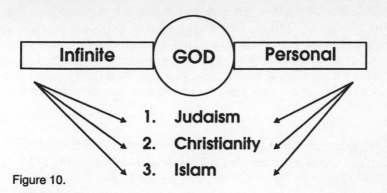

Figure 10.

One Critical Necessity

But how would each of these religions respond to the question, "How can I know if your God really exists?" Judaism and Islam would say that God has revealed Himself by "talking" to certain prophets, Moses, Mohammed, and others, who wrote down what He said in holy books. To accept their God, I would have to assume each writer's credibility. They said it was God who talked to them, and I just have to believe them.

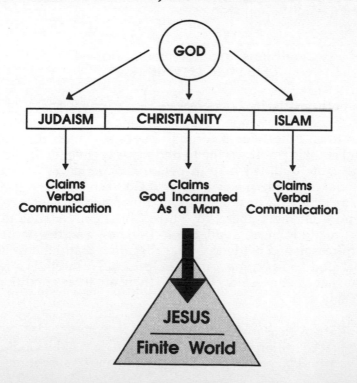

Christianity alone goes beyond the mere allegation that a God exists and "talks", to the claim that God came to earth as a physical man, Jesus Christ. Only Christianity claims that its founder is God incarnate, not a prophet or holy man. God became a human being and lived for more than thirty years in my triangle. No other religion offers such an opportunity to verify or falsify its claims.

"The Christian claim that the whole and only meaning of history before and after Christ rests on the historical appearance of Jesus Christ is a claim so strange, stupendous, and radical that it could not and cannot but contradict and upset the normal historical consciousness of ancient and modern times.
Karl Lowith, *Meaning in History*

Jesus either *is* or *is not* God as Christians claim him to be. You don't have to just believe this allegation. You can investigate this person using the normal rules of logic and reason. This is truly a testable hypothesis.

Conditions for a Reasonable Testing of the "God Hypothesis"

The Hypothesis Itself
I wish that my own pathway to finding God had been this clear. Rather, I meandered through books of philosophy, religion and autobiography trying to find my way. Eventually I did find the route outlined here in personal experience. For the reader who is wondering right now if God can be found, I believe I can save you considerable frustration and time. There is hope and excitement ahead for you. Christianity claims that God *has* made Himself available to be known in the natural world of reason and evidence. The allegation that the infinite-personal God had become a man as Jesus of Nazareth is a hypothesis that can be tested. To do so, there are three conditions that must be met.

Focusing In: A Reasonable Pursuit
The first condition is readily apparent. The visit by God occurred nearly 2000 years ago. How can anyone be sure it really

happened and that Jesus was a real person of history? To test the Christian claim will require reliance on the writings of the New Testament. My earlier view was that the gospel accounts contained legendary stories reworked over the centuries and distorted by translators, so that little remained of authentic history. In other words, I didn't believe the Bible was reliable. I felt that way even though I had never investigated the literary evidence concerning the New Testament's authenticity or its historical reliability.

The first condition, then, for a testing of the hypothesis concerning God was the need for a trustworthy first century historical record concerning Jesus. How else could anyone reasonably form a firsthand conviction concerning Jesus who was allegedly God if they had no eyewitness sources? So that will need to be the first pursuit; that is, to determine if the New Testament is reliable as a source of first century history.

A Method of Proof

In any intellectual pursuit there must be some means of fact gathering. Furthermore, there has to be some agreement on what would constitute an adequate proof of the God hypothesis? The scientific method was clearly the method of choice in observing the natural world. But it requires the experiment be repeatable in a controlled environment so it can be observed. History is not repeatable and does not lend itself to the scientific method. Neither do beauty, esthetic values, etc. How do you prove something that is a one-time event?

Fortunately, we routinely accept another method of proof for historical events. It is the legal method with our system of courts, judges and juries. A case of evidence is presented by the prosecution and the defense concerning the issue being tried. A judge or a jury weighs the evidence and makes a reasonable judgment or decision concerning the issue.

"I cannot make my peace with the randomness doctrine: I cannot abide the notion of purposelessness and blind chance in nature. And yet I do not know what to put in its place for the quieting of my mind...We talk—some of us anyway—about the absurdity of the human situation, but we do this because we do not know how we fit in, or what we are for."
Lewis Thomas, *On the Uncertainty of Science.*

This rational approach to gathering the data and weighing its validity is the way to approach the evidence concerning the New Testament and the person of Jesus. Since the New Testament claims to be a document of history, it must be examined using the legal method. You, the reader, will be both the judge and the jury of the evidence.

An Honest Skeptic

If faith in God is to be more than anti-intellectually and emotionally based, it has to be willing to test Biblical claims using the legal method. By this means it is able to scrutinize Christianity's claim that Jesus was the incarnation of God. But a third condition must be in place as well: honesty and objectivity before the evidence. The humorous story of a dishonest skeptic illustrates this point.

Once upon a time a man announced to his family, neighbors and co-workers that he was dead. When his wife took him to the local psychiatrist he was given the task of researching the medical school journals until he had a firm conviction on the question, Do dead people bleed? After weeks of reading he returned with the verdict that the evidence was overwhelming— dead people do not bleed. The psychiatrist smiled and grabbed a pin he had set aside for this very moment. He poked the man's finger, and waited for the man's response as several drops of blood dripped from his finger. The man turned ashen white and cried, "Amazing! Dead people do bleed after all!"

That man was a dishonest skeptic. Many want answers to questions about faith based on facts and evidence. It is equally important that their response to that evidence is honest. The pursuit to check out the God hypothesis would be futile if one's attitude was, "Don't confuse me with the facts. My mind is made up."

FOCUS & DISCUSSION —————————

1. What are some of the stereotypes of faith and/or Christians that you have or have noted in others? Why do you or others hold these views?
2. What intellectual factor do you think keeps more people from believing in God than any other? Why?
3. What other factors besides intellectual ones do you think keep people from believing in God.

4. How broad is the awareness among people of the problem of purpose and meaning? What are the ways in which people attempt to satisfy the need for purpose and meaning without God?
5. In what ways can you relate to the lack of fulfillment that comes with money, power, position, or prestige?
6. Explain how you might defend the statement: "Faith in God is reasonable."

TWO

CAN I BELIEVE THE BIBLE?

The Issue Of
Historical Reliability

*"The certainty of the existence of a God who would give
meaning to life has a far greater attraction than the knowledge
that without him one could do evil without being punished.
But there is no choice, and that is where the bitterness begins.
Confronted with this evil, confronted with death, man from
the very depths of his soul cries out for justice."*
    Albert Camus, *The Rebel*

"The test of truth is the known factual evidence..."
    Jacob Bronowski, *Science and Human Values.*

*O*ne of the most basic Christian truth claims is that Jesus
Christ was God in human flesh, the highest, most illuminating
revelation of God to man. Jesus revealed to all who knew Him,
by what He said and did, that He was the unique Son of God.
This is the hypothesis that we want to test.

The difficulty is not in recognizing the historical reality of a
man called Jesus of Nazareth, for that is assured by several recognized extra-Biblical sources.[1] The difficulty is that the only
detailed biography of this man Jesus are the Biblical gospel
sources of Matthew, Mark, Luke, and John. Are these records
credible, i.e., are they an authentic and historically reliable record of the words and deeds of Jesus?

A serious, yet amusing, commentary on this question was
written to syndicated columnist, Ann Landers. It is extreme
only in its wording, not in the ideas expressed.

Dear Ann: Please, for heaven's sake, stop pushing religion! Anyone with half a brain knows that your readers are, for the most part, simple-minded, superstitious dimwits who can't face life without a crutch. But doesn't it bother you when you advise about the laws of God — a 2,000-year-old fairy tale? One day I hope you write a column denouncing the God myth and then quit! The ultimate limit of human foolishness, the most preposterous bit of irrational hokum ever dreamed up by human kind is the baloney found in the scriptures. Such nonsense is for weaklings and idiots who are unable to think for themselves or accept responsibility for their own actions.[2]

If this commentary was valid, there would be no hope of forming a reasonable personal conviction concerning the allegation that Jesus was God. Does this writer have a point?

"I have never been interested in an historical Jesus. I should not care if it was proved by someone that the man called Jesus never lived, and that what was narrated in the Gospels was a figment of the writer's imagination. For the Sermon on the Mount would still be true for me."

Mahatma Gandhi

Testing the Authenticity of the New Testament Writings

Fortunately, the testing of ancient documents for authenticity is a common practice among literary scholars. There is a large body of literature, both earlier and later than the New Testament, where the issue of authenticity is also raised. For example, the histories of Herodotus and Caesar (5th and 1st centuries B.C., respectively) are well known. Tacitus and Josephus allegedly wrote histories of Rome and the Jews, respectively, about the end of the first century A.D. The criteria for testing such literature are known as the principles of historiography. Therefore, there is no need to create anything new for examination of the New Testament records, only apply already accepted tests.

Because this is unfamiliar ground for most, it is necessary to imagine an ancient scenario to understand the issues. There is a well-known work written about 50 B.C. entitled *Caesar's War Commentaries*.[3] They are the personal memoirs of Julius Caesar's brilliant military campaigns. Let us suppose shortly after they were written that a friend of Caesar was visiting the palace, noted the work, and requested a copy for his own library. Caesar granted his request, but there was no Xerox machine in his office. Instead, the friend needed to send for a trained copyist who would labor for days to handwrite every letter, word, and sentence. Would the copy be exactly like Caesar's original? That is unlikely.

Now a person visits the home of Caesar's friend, notes his copy, and secures permission to have his copyist come in to make a second generation copy for himself. Will it be exactly like the first generation copy? That is also unlikely. Furthermore, it is even less like Caesar's original. To the extent that changes occur in the copies, that is the extent to which they lack authenticity. So far the changes are probably minor, but multiply that scenario by hundreds of generations over centuries of time. The authenticity is certain to degenerate. By the time we reach the fifteenth century and put it on the printing press, only a shadow of Caesar's original writing may remain.

But why not just go to Caesar's original? Why rely on copies at all if we can go to the autograph (hand-written original)? The answer is simple: there are no autographs. Not only has Caesar's original never been found, but neither have the autographs of any other ancient document, including the New Testament writings. Therefore, we must work from whatever copies have been found, thereby requiring some guidelines to determine the degree of authenticity.

The Bibliographical Test

The bibliographical test addresses this very issue, that is, the accuracy of transmission over the centuries. Specifically, we need to know if the twentieth century Bible is an accurate reproduction of the first century Greek New Testament. There are three major questions that scholars ask of the literature in question to determine this.

1. *How Many Manuscripts Have Been Found?*

The first question concerns the number of manuscript copies, that is, the manuscript evidence. The more abundant the

number of ancient copies that are found, the better. Even if there
are variant readings, a large number of copies allows comparison and correlation in order to reproduce the original. Furthermore, a large number of manuscripts over the centuries
minimizes the possibility that a little band of people created the
documents "behind closed doors", so to speak. A large number
of copies means broader public exposure and greater accountability to integrity.

As a youth I knew virtually nothing about manuscript studies. My first exposure, though quite limited, came during college. In my skepticism, I remember thinking that it was
reasonably certain that the New Testament evidences would be
quite inferior to that of the writings of the great classical writers
such as Plato, Homer or Aristotle. Later in graduate school I discovered, to my surprise, that the New Testament was vastly superior. Additional study over the years since then has enhanced
my understanding of this academic discipline. These insights
are included throughout this chapter to give the reader a better
test scenario of our hypothesis.

How many manuscript copies of ancient works are available
for study today? Obviously, to know a work existed we would
need to have found at least one. The 643 manuscript copies that
exist of Homer's *Iliad* is the most for any ancient work. But this
is very unusual. There are only about 10 manuscripts ever
found of *Caesar's War Commentaries*, seven for Plato's *Tetralogies*,
twenty for Livy's *History of Rome*, and only a couple for Tacitus'
minor works.

What about the New Testament? There are more than 5300
known manuscripts in the original Greek language. There are,
in addition, more than 19,000 ancient New Testament manuscripts in Latin, Syriac, Armenian, and other language versions.
More than 24,000 hand-written copies of the New Testament
have survived. British scholar, F.F. Bruce, concludes from the
data that "There is no body of ancient literature in the world
which enjoys such a wealth of good textual attestation as the
New Testament."[4] Figure 1 shows the extreme contrast between
the manuscript evidence for the New Testament and that of
other ancient writings.

The comparison is not even close. So much for my reasonable certainty that the New Testament would not fare well
under scrutiny! When my reading during graduate school exposed me to these facts, I realized that I had been dishonest. I
never questioned, or even examined, the accuracy of the texts of

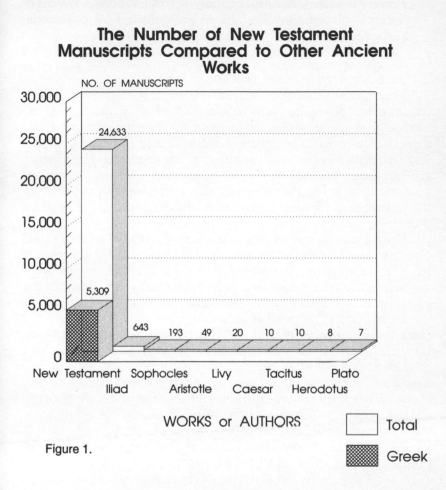

The Number of New Testament Manuscripts Compared to Other Ancient Works

Figure 1.

other works that I read. But I *knew* the New Testament text could not be trusted, and feigned intellectual reasons. However, my ignorance was the real culprit. Later in my career, when reading Sir Frederic Kenyon, eminent scholar of textual criticism, I found out that I had not been alone in holding this double standard:

> Scholars are satisfied that they possess substantially the true text of the principal Greek and Roman writers whose works have come down to us, of Sophocles, of Thucydides, of

Cicero, of Virgil; yet our knowledge of their writings depends on a mere handful of manuscripts, whereas the manuscripts of the New Testament are counted by hundreds, and even thousands.[5]

2. How Early Are The Manuscripts?

The second issue affecting transmission is the date at which the manuscript copies were written. Obviously, the further removed that these copies were from the originals in time, the more likely to include errors, additions and deletions, i.e., be less authentic. Fortunately, while the chance for copyist's errors are increased because of the large number of New Testament manuscripts, these manuscripts also increase proportionately the means of correcting such errors and recovering the original wording.

How close to the originals do ancient works actually get? *Caesar's War Commentaries* was written about 50 B.C., yet we have no manuscripts available for study today which were written before the 9th century — a gap of over 900 years. Most of the Greek writings have even greater gaps (1000-1500 years), while the Latin writers somewhat less. The shortest span of any ancient work is probably that of Virgil, about 300 years between his writing and the oldest copy known. However, such a short time period is not at all typical. Many people that I talk to find troublesome the fact that there are no preserved copies of any classical work for several hundred years after the date of original composition. But they are equally astonished when they see the data concerning the New Testament.

It is generally agreed that the New Testament writings were penned over a fifty-year period, beginning at approximately A.D. 47. For ease in calculations, I will use the year A.D. 100 as the latest possible date for their completion. What is the earliest copy ever found? The range for all other literature is 300 to more than 1500 years. The John Rylands papyrus, dating about A.D. 125, is a fragment containing a few verses of the New Testament gospel of John. This is only some 35 years after the original gospel had been written by the apostle. Whoever used this copy could have known the author, or even been personally taught by the apostle John, himself.

However, a find consisting of a majority of the records of the New Testament would be needed to do textual studies. The Bodmer and Chester Beatty papyri, dating from about A.D. 175-250, exceeds every demand. Here are major copies within 100-

150 years of the originals. Kenyon's commentary on the significance of these manuscripts contradicts many people's perception of what is true regarding the New Testament records.

> The net result of this discovery...is, in fact, to reduce the gap between the earlier manuscripts and the traditional dates of the New Testament books so far that it becomes negligible in any discussion of their authenticity. No other ancient book has anything like such early and plentiful testimony to its text, and no unbiased scholar would deny that the text that has come down to us is substantially sound.[6]

Figure 2 compares several ancient works with the New Testament in regard to the time interval between the original and extant copies.

The Time Interval Between the Date of Writing and the Earliest Known Manuscript of the New Testament Compared to Other Ancient Works

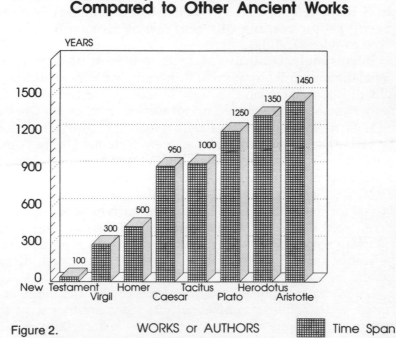

Figure 2. WORKS or AUTHORS ▨ Time Span

Again, the New Testament stands far above all other ancient writings in manuscript evidence and short time span. There was a nearly continuous chain of copies from the originals to the

printing press. If the text was not essentially like the autographs, when could they have become corrupted? We have copies in every century back to the beginning. Based on this
evidence, the conclusion of scholar F.F. Bruce is certainly
justified:

> The evidence for our New Testament writings is ever so
> much greater than the evidence for many writings of classi-
> cal authors, the authenticity of which no-one dreams of
> questioning. And if the New Testament were a collection of
> secular writings, their authenticity would generally be re-
> garded as beyond all doubt.[7]

3. How Accurately Were The Manuscripts Copied?

The final question of the bibliographical test measures the
extent of distortion of the text over the centuries. I have already
shared my earlier contention that the text of the New Testament
was quite hopelessly muddled by insertions, interpretations,
etc. Scholars refer to this as distortion of the meaning of the text.
Several people reading different manuscripts will arrive at
diverse understandings.

Interestingly, Dr. Bruce Metzger, professor of New Testament language and literature at Princeton, has published the results of his research on this very question. He compared the
many manuscripts of three ancient works: a religious work of
the ancient Greeks, Homer's *Iliad*, a religious book of Hinduism,
the *Mahabharata*, and the Christian New Testament.[8] The copies
of the three works were divided into lines of ten words each to
make the comparison easier. The works varied in length from
15,600 lines for the *Iliad*, 20,000 for the New Testament, and
250,000 for the *Mahabharata*. Variations such as spelling differences, word order, etc., that did not affect the meaning of the
text, were ignored. All differences in the manuscripts affecting
the reader's understanding were counted. How much distortion did he find?

Dr. Metzger reported that 764 lines of the *Iliad* were corrupted, a distortion rate of about 5%. Said another way, the
meaning of one out of every twenty lines is uncertain. Which
Iliad do we read in literature class? Who decided which manuscript was correct? Yet, it is probably rare that an instructor
would caution students about the authenticity of the Iliad when
it is assigned or discussed. The authenticity is assumed.

The *Mahabharata* was even worse with at least 26,000 lines corrupted, somewhat more than a 10% distortion rate. One out of every ten lines of this religious book was "up for grabs," so to speak. This is not a very good source on which to trust your life or destiny!

The data for the New Testament is incredible. Only 40 lines, or 1/5 of 1% (0.2%), are distorted. This is twenty-five times more accurately copied than the *Iliad*, which is considered good. Besides, F.F. Bruce has said that "the variant readings about which any doubt remains among textual critics of the New Testament affect no material question of historic fact or of Christian faith and practice."[9] Where was the New Testament textual confusion that had made it unacceptable to me back in my college years? Figure 3 summarizes Metzger's research results.

A Comparison of the Rate of Distortion of Manuscripts Due to Copying Errors

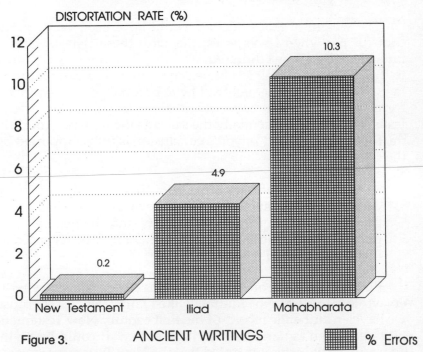

Figure 3.

4. *The Evidence of Quotes in Manuscript Writings Other Than the New Testament*

Furthermore, the extant writings of the church Fathers of the first three centuries after Christ contain over 36,000 quotations or allusions to the New Testament books. This makes it possible to reconstruct the New Testament text from them alone. Indeed, Metzger says that "so extensive are these citations that if all other sources for our knowledge of the text of the New Testament were destroyed, they would be sufficient alone for the reconstruction of practically the entire New Testament." Kenyon's conclusion is justified by the evidence:

> It cannot be too strongly asserted that in substance the text of the Bible is certain: Especially is this the case with the New Testament. The number of manuscripts of the New Testament, of early translations from it, and of quotations from it in the oldest writers of the Church, is so large that it is practically certain that the true reading of every doubtful passage is preserved in some one or other of these ancient authorities. This can be said of no other ancient book in the world.[10]

The weight of this evidence would have been very significant for me when I was wrestling with these issues. Unfortunately, at that time I didn't know about it. But it was exposure to this evidence during graduate school that began a revolution in my thinking. Subsequently, I have become persuaded that if I grabbed my current copy of the New Testament records of Jesus' life, that it is essentially the same as the writers wrote it in the first century A.D. Kenyon's conclusion is fully supported by the scientific facts:

> ...the last foundation for any doubt that the Scriptures have come down to us substantially as they were written has now been removed. Both the authenticity and the general integrity of the books of the New Testament may be regarded as finally established.[11]

But how can someone know that what the first-century writers wrote is true? Maybe Matthew liked fairy tales. Just because we have an authentic record of the first century New Testament writings doesn't guarantee that it is history. It could be myth. So far I have only demonstrated that the New Testament in comparison with all other ancient writings has 1) more manuscripts, 2) earlier manuscripts, and 3) is more accurately copied. But how can a person know that what they wrote about really happened as they described it?

Testing the Historical Reliability
of the New Testament

Testing the truthfulness of the New Testament records requires some independent sources that would substantiate its historical accuracy. There is also a need to learn more about the New Testament documents and their authors within the historical context of the first century. Are the documents internally consistent? These are issues addressed routinely in literary criticism. The procedures for testing these matters may be divided into two areas, the external and internal evidence tests.

External Evidence Test

It is well-known that there are many references in the New Testament records to allegedly historical people (e.g., Pontius Pilate, Gallio, and Caesar Augustus), places (e.g., Jericho, Egypt, and the Sea of Galilee), and events (Roman census, crucifixion of Jesus, and a Palestinian drought). Indeed, Luke, traditional author of one of the gospels and the Acts of the Apostles, consistently casts his writings in alleged historical context, for example: "In the fifteenth year of the reign of Tiberius Caesar—when Pontius Pilate was governor of Judea, Herod tetrarch of Galilee, his brother Philip tetrarch of Iturea and Traconitis, and Lysanias tetrarch of Abilene — during the high priesthood of Annas and Caiaphas ..."[12] This is a real plus for our test purposes, as scholar F. F. Bruce points out: "A writer who thus relates his story to the wider context of world history is courting trouble if he is not careful; he affords his critical readers so many opportunities for testing his accuracy. Luke takes this risk and stands the test admirably."[13] We want to find out what evidence led him to that conclusion.

The Evidence of Archaeology

One of the most fruitful sources in this regard is the findings in the field of archaeology. Volumes have been written on specific details, mostly in this century. Scientific archaeology is really only a century and a half old. British scientists first pioneered the modern techniques that have led to a revolution of knowledge about ancient times. Perhaps it is safe to say that because of modern archaeology, more is known today about first century New Testament background than anyone has known about it since the third century. With so much data available today, it is no longer difficult to test the New Testament's claim to historicity.

Politarchs. During the apostle Paul's second missionary journey he visited the city of Thessalonica. Luke refers to the city magistrates there by the term "politarchs."[14] The problem is that this title does not occur anywhere in other literature, and it was assumed that Luke coined the term because he did not have first-hand knowledge of the area. Obviously this was an alleged example of the New Testament's sloppy history. But beginning with William Ramsay in the late 19th century, at least nineteen inscriptions have been found by archaeologists which cite "politarchs" as the correct title of magistrates in Macedonian towns. Luke was historically right. Indeed, F. F. Bruce says that Luke's "sure familiarity with the proper titles of all the notable persons who are mentioned in his pages" is "one of the most remarkable tokens of his accuracy."[15] He cites several pages of examples. After a lifetime of research, archaeologist William Ramsay, classical scholar and archaeologist at Oxford, acknowledged that the evidence changed his mind from one of skepticism and unbelief to the view "that Luke's history is unsurpassed in respect of its trustworthiness." He identified Luke as "a historian of the first rank," placing him "along with the very greatest of historians."

Crucifixion of Jesus. The gospel writers refer to the use of nails in the crucifixion of Jesus on a cross of wood. The use of nails, as opposed to tying the victim on the cross, and even the practice of crucifixion in Palestine, has been questioned by critics. Surely the writers embellished their stories with unhistorical details. A recent publication suggests not. I read with fascination a scientific article reporting on the excavation of the only crucifixion victim ever discovered. The 24-28 year old man was found in a tomb near Jerusalem with a 7 1/2-inch-long nail through his feet. His crucifixion was dated by the carbon-14 method at A.D. 42 (Jesus was crucified about A.D. 30). Furthermore, the calf bones were "brutally fractured...clearly produced by a single, strong blow." This was amazing evidence supporting a Palestinian variation of Roman crucifixion referred to in the gospel of John: "The soldiers therefore came and broke the legs of the first man who had been crucified with Jesus, and then those of the other. But when they came to Jesus and found that he was already dead, they did not break his legs."[16] The archaeologist explains:

Normally, the Romans left the crucified person undisturbed to die slowly of sheer physical exhaustion leading to asphyxia. However, Jewish tradition required burial on the day of execution. Therefore, in Palestine the executioner would break the legs of the crucified person in order to hasten his death and thus permit burial before nightfall. This practice, described in the Gospels in reference to the two thieves ... has now been archaeologically confirmed.[17]

Roman Census. Nearly everything that I have read over the years in the field of archaeology seems to confirm the trustworthiness of biblical statements. The census referred to by Luke which took Joseph and Mary to Bethlehem to be registered is now known to be something the Roman Empire did every fourteen years beginning with Augustus, and can be reconciled with the biblical date of their journey.[18]

Pontius Pilate. Pilate, identified in the New Testament gospel accounts as the governor of Judea at the time of Christ's crucifixion, squares with references to him in writings of the Jewish historian Josephus and the Roman historian Tacitus. Archaeological excavation of the site of ancient Caesarea, the city from which he ruled, uncovered a 2 x 3 foot cornerstone with the inscription: "Pontius Pilate, the Prefect of Judea, has dedicated to the people of Caesarea a temple in honor of Tiberius."[19]

Legal Proceedings. The legal proceedings against Jesus and Paul mentioned in the trial narratives of the New Testament correspond exactly to what we know of Roman practice during that period of the first century A.D.[20] F.F. Bruce extends the accuracy even "to the more general sphere of local colour and atmosphere. He [Luke] gets the atmosphere right every time."[21]

Sodom and Gomorrah. The Old Testament writings also proved true when checked against external evidence. The ancient cities of Sodom and Gomorrah, according to the book of Genesis, were judged and destroyed by God.[22] Because these cities had never been found or identified in any other literature, they were viewed as teaching a moral lesson but were not actual historical places. But now they are known to be very real places according to excavations at Ebla, a city in northern Syria dating from the third and early second centuries B.C. Inscriptions on some of the more than 20,000 tablets found there refer to the cities of Sodom and Gomorrah as trading partners of Ebla.[23]

> *"A young man who wishes to remain a sound Atheist cannot be too careful of his reading. There are traps everywhere—'Bibles laid open, millions of surprises,' as Herbert says, 'fine nets and strategems.' God is, if I might say it, very unscrupulous."*
> C.S. Lewis, *Surprised by Joy*

Hittites. The Hittites, entirely unknown except for references in the Old Testament writings, were thought to be fictitious or erroneously named. But twentieth century archaeology has now confirmed that such a people did exist and once occupied much of modern Turkey.[24]

The Testimony of Scholars

The professional judgments of international experts also support the historical accuracy of the New Testament. William Albright, famous archaeologist of Johns Hopkins University, writes:

> The excessive skepticism shown toward the Bible by important schools of the eighteenth and nineteenth centuries, certain phases of which still appear periodically, has been progressively discredited. Discovery after discovery has established the accuracy of innumerable details, and has brought increased recognition to the value of the Bible as a source of history.[25]

This theme is repeated again and again. For example, Millar Burrows of Yale states that "archaeological work has unquestionably strengthened confidence in the reliability of the Scriptural record. More than one archaeologist has found his respect for the Bible increased by the experience of excavation in Palestine."[26] This is a real challenge for those who demand evidence. If they don't believe the truthfulness of New Testament statements, they can get a spade and check it out! Nelson Glueck, renowned Jewish archaeologist, claims that "no archaeological discovery has ever controverted a biblical reference."[27]

Finally, Kenyon, considered a foremost authority in this field, expressed what some have thought was an overly optimistic statement: "Archaeology has not yet said its last word, but the results already achieved confirm what faith would suggest, that the Bible can do nothing but gain from an increase in knowledge."[28] While this was said over fifty years ago, Kitchen recently affirmed that the "continuing discoveries and work of the intervening decades have not changed, merely enhanced, the truth of his judgment."[29] So much for my youthful view that Christianity and faith were anti-intellectual.

Internal Evidence Test

Somewhere in my early years I picked up the view that the stories written about Jesus were really legends that had developed long after he was gone. During my college skepticism, I maintained that it was naive to accept 2000-year-old accounts if they were not written by those who lived at the same time as Jesus, and by those who knew him personally. I couldn't imagine a better source than someone who was actually there.

Eye-Witness Authors

Partly at that time, and extensively later, I discovered that this is exactly what the New Testament writings claim for themselves, i.e., they were written by eyewitnesses or had eyewitness sources. Furthermore, the Gospel accounts of the words and deeds of Jesus were being preached within fifty days and had limited circulation in written form within twenty-five years after his death and resurrection. The apostle Peter was able to stand in Jerusalem less than two months after Jesus' death, with those hostile to the Christian movement present, and say, "Men of Israel, listen to these words: 'Jesus the Nazarene, a man attested to you by God with miracles and wonders and signs which God performed through Him in your midst, just as you yourselves know....'" He went on to say that "this Jesus God raised up again, to which we are all witnesses,"[30] and there is no indication of any attempts to rebut these appeals to history. Indeed, no one has yet been able to do so.

Imagine the difficulties today of trying to publish a totally fabricated biography of former president John F. Kennedy. In this account JFK is depicted as walking on water, healing the sick in front of crowds, raising the dead, and feeding 5000 people with five barley loaves and two fish. Following his death he was said to be resurrected and he ascended to heaven before over 500 eyewitnesses. As a result, a massive religious movement has begun in which JFK is worshipped.

The only way this "biography" could be accepted by the public is if the book never fell into the hands of anyone who knew Mr. Kennedy, or if all who ever knew him were dead. Otherwise, those who knew him would testify that it was untrue. If there were still a few hardy "believers" in JFK, his body could be exhumed which would put an end to all such nonsense.

Likewise, if there was any fabrication or departure from the facts about Jesus on Peter's part, it would be inconceivable that 3000 would respond in repentance and faith to a person they knew to be a fraud or product of Peter's imagination.[31] If Peter knew his statements about Jesus were false, surely he was smart enough to leave Jerusalem and go where people had no first-hand knowledge of Jesus. But Christian teaching about Jesus was successful where the people were in the best position to demonstrate its possible historical falsehood.

"Faith is not blind...In the case of Christian faith it arose for the earliest disciples from historical contemporaneity with Jesus. They were not compelled by the evidence: plenty of people saw it and declined to commit themselves. But the evidence was the ground on which they committed themselves.
Michael Green, *The Truth of God Incarnate*

The apostle Paul, too, with his life on the line before the Roman procurator Festus and King Agrippa, appealed to the events of Jesus' life as historically true. He said "the king knows about these matters, and I speak to him with confidence, since I am persuaded that none of these things escaped his notice: for this has not been done in a corner."[32]

Early Date of Writing
Furthermore, the early dating of the New Testament documents within 20-30 years after Jesus' death made the theory of legends untenable. As Bruce says, "the disciples could not afford to risk inaccuracies (not to speak of willful manipulation of the facts), which would at once be exposed by those who would be only too glad to do so."[33] No legend is known to have developed within the same generation as the events and persons themselves.[34]

A Highly Probable Verdict

Based on the very methods that literary and historical scholars use today, the only reasonable and logical conclusion that I can draw is that the Bible is the most reliable book of antiquity. If anyone chooses to reject the New Testament evidence as insufficient, honesty to the facts requires that they reject all other ancient literature as well, whose evidence is quite inferior to that supporting the New Testament. For me, only my remaining prejudices caused me to stubbornly cling to my former skeptical views. Had I only known then the more complete evidence that I gained later and have included in this chapter, I do not believe my search would have been as prolonged.

"Prejudices are rarely overcome by argument; not being founded in reason they cannot be destroyed by logic."
Tryon Edwards, *The New Dictionary of Thoughts.*

In the 18th century the French skeptic Voltaire boasted that within one hundred years of his time the Bible and Christianity would be swept into obsolescence and pass into history. Instead, about fifty years after his death the Geneva Bible Society took over his press and his house to produce stacks of Bibles and distribute them around the world.[35] It is hard to ignore or destroy reliable history!

C.S. Lewis, professor of Medieval and Renaissance Literature at Cambridge University, acknowledged that the evidence for the historicity of the Gospels was a major factor in his conversion from atheism.[36] Frank Morison, an English journalist, set out to prove that the story of Christ was encumbered with legend and myth. He found by his research that the biblical records were historically valid.[37] Scores of others have searched the historical evidence and found it exceedingly convincing.

We have examined some of the evidence supporting the second and crucial condition for testing the God hypothesis; that is, the need for a trustworthy first-century historical record concerning Jesus. The reader is now in the position to be the judge on this matter. We must now turn our focus on what these historically reliable documents report about what Jesus of Nazareth said and did. To determine if He was more than a man will require that we examine the primary sources for the data concerning his life. The jury, as far as that matter is concerned, is still out.

FOCUS & DISCUSSION ————————————————

1. Why is it so important for the argument of God's existence that the New Testament is a trustworthy first century historical record?
2. What evidence in this chapter was the most unexpected to you? ...the most significant to altering your understanding of the New Testament? Why?
3. How well-known in society today is the evidence for the authenticity and historical reliability of the New Testament presented in this chapter? ...among the Christian community? Why do you think this is so?
4. What evidence weakens the allegation that the New Testament accounts of Jesus are only legends?
5. Suppose you were a participant in an event that occurred 25-30 years ago. Can you remember the incident sufficiently to recognize a fabrication of the event if related to you verbally or in print? What implications does this have to the claim that the gospel accounts are fabricated legends, not historically true?

THREE
IS JESUS REALLY GOD?
A Look At The Evidence

The Archbishop of Canterbury: "Jesus is the Son of God, you know."
Jane Fonda: "Maybe he is for you, but he's not for me."
Archbishop: "Well, either he is or he isn't."
   Conversation on the Dick Cavett Show
   (in *The Quest for Faith*, C. Stephen Evans)

When a person stops believing in God, he does not believe in nothing.
He will believe in anything.
   G.K. Chesterton, British writer

J esus faced a most difficult task. He was born into a Jewish family 2000 years ago. He grew up in the small town of Nazareth in Israel, a remote and unimportant province of the Roman empire. By every known indication he appeared to be a normal boy to those who knew him. However, when he was about thirty years of age he stood up in the synagogue of his home town and announced, "There is some thing I have been meaning to tell you — I'm God!"

If one of my friends or colleagues were to make such a statement, I would either laugh or cry. I would assume he was joking or had lost his mind! What makes Jesus' statement any different? The only way that I could seriously consider such a claim is if he provided some powerful evidence to back it up. I would need some reasons to prove the guy credible. That is where we are in our test as well. Fortunately, we have every reason to trust the New Testament documents as a reliable source of history. The claim that Jesus was God now needs to be tested to determine its validity.

What I am proposing is familiar territory to me. In my professional expertise of ecology, I would occasionally take my students into the field to give them first-hand experience with the lecture subject. That's what I am going to suggest we do with Jesus' claim — take a field trip. We can then test Jesus' credibility for ourselves by observing his claims and actions via a walk through the accounts written by eyewitnesses.

Testing the Hypothesis: God Became a Man

Evidences of Jesus' Claims

Messiah.[1] The words that I used above for Jesus' announcement in his hometown were not those quoted in the Scriptures. Indeed, it could correctly be argued that on that occasion he did not claim deity at all. The incident as recorded in the physician Luke's account indicates that Jesus read from the Old Testament book of the prophet Isaiah.[2] This was a very familiar prophecy that the Jews maintained would be fulfilled by the Messiah or Christ when he came. Jesus concluded His reading with the words, "Today this Scripture has been fulfilled in your hearing." In other words, Jesus said, "Here I am, ready or not!" Jesus here claimed to be the prophesied Messiah, who was not necessarily divine (though see the note).[3]

Nevertheless, this is a strong claim, and one that he made on other occasions as well.[4] The response of the people who heard him that day makes this clear: "Is not this Joseph's son?" Their questioning prompted Jesus to anticipate what would be a reasonable expectation under the circumstances when He said, "No doubt you will quote this proverb to me, 'Physician, heal yourself...'" This was equivalent to our modern expression, 'Prove it'. It is clear from the context that the people rejected, temporarily at least, Jesus' claim to be the Messiah. Who is right? Only additional evidence can answer this question.

Lord God.[5] Whether or not Jesus was the Messiah paled, however, compared to the issue raised in an encounter that Jesus had with the Pharisees. In it he challenged their teaching that the Messiah was to have only a human nature. Matthew records his reasoning:

Now while the Pharisees were gathered together, Jesus asked them a question, saying, "What do you think about the Christ, whose son is He?" They said to Him, "The son of David." He said to them, "Then how does David in the Spirit call Him 'Lord,' saying, 'The Lord said to My Lord'... If David then calls Him 'Lord', how is He his son?" And no one was able to answer Him a word...

The point of the question is that if David in the Old Testament psalm refers to his physical descendant, the Messiah, by the name of God, then how can they teach anything less than a divine Messiah? The phrase David used is *"Yahweh* said to *Adonai."* Both are names of God, but he applies the second one to his descendant who would be the Messiah. Why would Jesus bring this up except to correct an oversight in their teaching concerning his nature? Clearly he wanted them to understand that as their Messiah he was both man and God.

I AM.[6] But why was Jesus so subtle? Had He ever come right out and say He was God? That did happen on an occasion when the Jewish leadership asked him point blank, "whom do you make yourself out to be?" Among other things Jesus said, "Truly, truly, I say to you, before Abraham was born, I AM." Included in His response was the claim of preexistence, that is, He lived before Abraham, who lived about 2000 years earlier. Being born a baby in Bethlehem was not His beginning. Indeed, the way He phrased his answer in the present tense suggests that He had no beginning at all.

More importantly, Jesus applied to Himself the title, "I AM." This was one of the names of God from the Old Testament.[7] For a man to do this was unprecedented. The Jewish contemporaries of Jesus were reluctant to even *say* the name of God for fear that their unclean lips may defile it. But Jesus not only put it on His lips, He put it on His nametag as well.

The context also supports this view. Upon hearing His answer, they attempted to stone Jesus to death. This is clear evidence that they understood Him to be claiming deity, since only such an allegedly blasphemous claim would warrant death according to their law.

One with the Father.[8] That was not the only time Jesus was asked to clear up his identity. At the winter Feast of Dedication in Jerusalem, he was asked again, "How long will you keep us in suspense? If you are the Christ, tell us plainly." Jesus responded, "I and the Father are one." What could he mean?

One possibility is that the Father and Jesus are 'one and the same.' This would mean that while Jesus was on earth, there was no one home upstairs. They are the same person. The grammar of the Greek is helpful here. "One" would need to be in the masculine gender if this was the intended meaning. It is not. It is in the neuter gender.

The neuter gender could mean to be 'in agreement' or 'in unity.' This would be somewhat equivalent to my saying I was in the will of God. But the context of the passage is against that. There is nothing in this interpretation that could possibly justify the death penalty, which they attempted by stoning.

The contemporaries of Jesus, who spoke the same language and shared the same culture, were in the best position to know what he meant by 'one.' Their understanding is clearly stated, "For a good work we do not stone you, but for blasphemy; and because you, being a man, make yourself out to be God." 'One' here means 'essence', that is, Jesus shares all the divine attributes of the Father. This fits the grammar and the context perfectly.

From Above and Not of this World.[9] During the years of my search for answers, I recall thinking that Jesus was, for the most part, quite like any other man. For example, his conversation was wise but wasn't indicative of a claim to deity. I questioned why anyone bothered to attribute deity to Him at all. In hindsight, I realize that I took that position because of ignorance, that is, I really was not acquainted enough with Jesus' teaching to know any better. When I began to read the gospel records, I realized that many of his statements could never appropriately be a part of anyone else's conversation.

Try, for example, to use some of Jesus' words as your own with a neighbor across the backyard fence: "You are from below, I am from above..." You would certainly have his attention. To add, "you are of this world; I am not of this world," may send your neighbor running — to call 911! These are not the statements of an ordinary man. To claim to be from another world and to add, besides, that unless people believe you are God ("I Am") they will die unforgiven is to court disaster — unless you can gain credibility by backing your claims up somehow.

Give Eternal Life to Anyone.[10] Imagine yourself sitting at a rest island in a busy shopping mall. You beckon several people to you and, with discreetness, ask if they would like to live forever. Caught off guard, they just stare back at you. You assure them that if, after further thought, eternal life sounds like a good plan, they should look you up and you will grant it to them. I doubt that you would be overwhelmed by the traffic jam at your front door.

Jesus said that he could give eternal life to whomever he wished. To Martha and Mary, devastated by the death of their brother, Lazarus, Jesus said, "I am the resurrection and the life; he who believes in me shall live even if he dies, and everyone who lives and believes in me shall never die." What makes the difference between his saying it or me saying it? Nothing, unless one of us can provide evidence that he can really do it. Jesus did — he raised Lazarus from the dead.

All Authority in Heaven and on Earth.[11] If you want to give your spouse or your boss at work a little lightness in their day, ask for a private conference to talk. Sit directly in front of your spouse or boss, look them directly in the eyes, and say, "All authority has been given to me in heaven and on earth." This is another of Jesus' ordinary human statements. I believe it is well within the mark to suggest that if much of what Jesus said were put into our mouth, we would be prime candidates to be locked up or given psychological treatment. Indeed, Jesus did die for who he claimed to be. Throughout history people have been sentenced for what they do, i.e., for a crime committed. But Jesus was crucified for who He claimed to be: "...He ought to die because He made Himself out to be the Son of God."[12]

A SUMMARY OF SOME OF JESUS' CLAIMS TO BE GOD

1. **Messiah** (Christ) - "Mighty God" and "Everlasting Father" in Isaiah 9:6
2. **Lord God** - "Adonai"
3. **I AM** - Eternal One
4. **One with the Father** - Essence: Possesses all the divine attributes
5. **From above and not of the world** - Heavenly origin
6. **Can give eternal life to anyone** - Conqueror of death
7. **Has all authority in heaven and on earth** - Highest and ultimate authority

Figure 1.

There can be little doubt from our field trip thus far, that Jesus claimed to be God. The data of His life from history is quite convincing. Albert Schweitzer, who himself believed that Jesus misunderstood his own nature, nevertheless acknowledged that the evidence for His claim to be God was good. The concern of his M.D. dissertation at Strasborg in France was how Jesus could be sane and claim to be God.[13] Figure 1 summarizes the evidence of Jesus' claims.

Evidences of Jesus' Actions

Many have claimed to be god. Hindu holy men can even hold crowds with magical powers. Invariably, however, their lives fall short of deity and they are no longer credible to their followers. Jesus is the exception. The more time people spent with him, the more certain they were that his claims were valid. This is where the idea of a field trip is particularly valuable. We can see Jesus through the eyes of those who walked with him. Luke recorded the history of what Jesus did for approximately two years following the people's rejection of his claim in Nazareth. During those two years many changed their minds about him. The contrast from skepticism to acceptance is striking. What changed their minds?

The answer to that question is obvious to anyone who takes seriously the history in the biblical accounts of Jesus' life. The eyewitnesses report things he did that were astounding. Many of his contemporaries were persuaded by these events to believe in his divine nature, though they were predisposed against such a conclusion. If we are willing, we can now look for ourselves at what they saw him do. We will continue our field trip.

Authority to Forgive and Remove the Consequences of Sin[14]

Several of the events that Luke recorded in his gospel are intriguing. Following his announcement in Nazareth, Jesus went to Capernaum on the northwest shoreline of the Sea of Galilee. There, in what was likely the apostle Peter's home, many of Israel's most capable religious leaders — Pharisees and lawyers — had gathered. Because the crowd limited access, some men carrying a paralyzed man on a stretcher, presented him to Jesus through a hole in the roof. Jesus immediately responded, "Friend, your sins are forgiven you." The scribes and Pharisees found that offensive: "Who is this man who speaks blasphemies? Who can forgive sins, but God alone?" What was it that caused their offense?

Imagine that, while I was speaking to a group, one individual jumped up, rushed to the podium, and knocked me down with a hard blow. Promptly he had a change of heart, apologized profusely, and begged my forgiveness. If I granted it, would the rest of my audience likely accuse me of blasphemy — usurping the prerogative of God? Not only is that unlikely, but they would probably commend me for my benevolence. Somehow, the circumstances in Jesus' situation must have been different than those in the imaginary one that I described. Let me try again.

Once again someone in my audience nearly knocks me out, and apologizes for it. But before I can respond, someone else from my audience comes forward and says to the one who hit me, "I want you to know that I forgive you for that." Even in my dazed condition, I would question what this third party has to do with it — I was the one that got hit. By offering forgiveness this third party was taking both my position and my right. To the Pharisees and lawyers, Jesus was the third party. It is unlikely that he ever saw this man before. The man did nothing to him. Whatever sin the paralyzed man had in his life was a matter between him and God. That is why the religious leaders were reasoning that Jesus was guilty of blasphemy in that He, a third party, claimed the position and right of God.

Furthermore, they were thinking that his talk was cheap. They didn't believe that He actually removed the man's sin. After all, it is rather difficult to demonstrate that you have forgiven someone's sins. But there was a way in this case. Luke records Jesus' response to the challenge:

"But in order that you may know that the Son of Man has authority on earth to forgive sins," He said to the paralytic, "I say to you, rise, and take up your stretcher and go home." And at once he rose up before them, and took up what he had been lying on, and went home, glorifying God. And they were all seized with astonishment ... saying, "We have seen remarkable things today."[15]

To instantly heal a paralyzed man and send him home carrying his bed is in itself arresting. But how did this prove that Jesus had taken away the man's sins? The erudite group present there seemed quite persuaded. The answer is found in understanding a certain conviction of the Jews of that day; that is, they saw a direct relationship between sin and consequent judgment in the form of pain, suffering, etc. In the form of an equation, they would say:

Presence of Sin ——— Leads to ——➤ Consequence of Sin

In other words, if I were climbing a stairs with a group of first century Jewish peers, and hurt myself in a fall, they would gather around and ask me what sin I had committed recently! This mindset is illustrated even by Jesus' disciples on another occasion when they asked Jesus whether the plight of a man *born* blind was caused by his parent's sin or his own.[16] Therefore, when the paralyzed man on the stretcher was brought to Jesus, the religious authorities saw his paralysis as a consequence of his sin. This afforded Jesus an opportunity to visibly demonstrate, to their satisfaction, the removal of the man's sin, i.e., by healing him. If the presence of sin caused the presence of paralysis, the removal of paralysis meant the removal of the sin that caused it.

Removal of the Sin ◀——— Proves ——— Removal of the
   that caused it   Consequence of Sin

The Pharisees and lawyers responded, "We have seen remarkable things today." While Jesus used such logic to satisfy their need for overt evidence that day, he did not actually share their simplistic view of the consequences of sin.[17]

Authority over Death[18]
At the southern Galilean city of Nain, Jesus met a procession enroute to taking a widow's only son to burial. Jesus' action is recorded by Luke.

And when the Lord saw her, He felt compassion for her, and said to her, "Do not weep." And He came up and touched the coffin; and the bearers came to a halt. And He said, "Young man, I say to you, arise!" And the dead man sat up, and began to speak. And Jesus gave him back to his mother. And fear gripped them all...

Fear indeed. Had I been present when the young man stood up in his coffin, I would have needed a place to sit down! Jesus had compassion for the widow, and raised her son from the dead. Many others present that day had compassion, too, but all they could do was weep. The gulf between the two is immense. The only way this incident would not revolutionize a person's view of Jesus is if they denied that it ever happened. But on what basis? These are the most reliable records of antiquity. The people who saw this miracle that day realized that Jesus was special as indicated by their comments that "A great prophet has arisen among us!" and "God has visited His people!" Joseph's boy never did things like *this* before. It was getting harder and harder for His contemporaries to refer to Him as only the carpenter's son.

Authority over Nature[19]

Jesus and his disciples were crossing the Sea of Galilee when a sudden, severe wind, familiar to Galilean fishermen yet today, threatened their lives. In the midst of his disciples' panic, Jesus "rebuked the wind and the surging waves, and they stopped, and it became calm." Jesus' mastery over natural elements was so instant and decisive, that those who were with him appropriately asked, "Who then is this, that He commands even the winds and the water, and they obey Him?" That is the crucial question.

Could Jesus, as a human teacher only, forgive sin, heal the body, raise the dead, and command nature to obey him? Perhaps he was like the prophet Elijah who, as a human, also did miraculous acts. But there was a significant difference between the two that would have been very evident to the Jews especially. It was characteristic of all the prophets to preface or conclude all they did with a "Thus saith the Lord" or "Thus the Lord did." But Jesus said, "I am the Resurrection and the Life", "I give eternal life," and "I have all authority in heaven and earth". To be a prophet, he would have to be a liar.[20]

"Ultimately, the problem of the meaning of history revolves around the question: 'Who is man himself and what is his origin and final destination?' Outside the central biblical revelation of creation, the fall into sin and redemption through Jesus Christ, no real answer is to be found to this question..."

Herman Dooyerweerd,
Dutch professor of philosophy

Many Other Convincing Proofs

It was Jesus' strategy to give reasons for people to believe in him. His invitation was clear: "Do not believe me unless I do what my Father does. But if I do it, even though you do not believe me, believe the miracles..."[21] That is what we have been looking at, i.e., the miracles of Jesus. In addition, as a result of recent study, I have noticed other indications of Jesus' deity in the records as well.

Acceptance of Worship.[22] Before Jesus began his public ministry, he experienced forty days of temptation. When invited to worship the devil in exchange for an earthly kingdom, Jesus quoted the Law, "You shall worship the Lord your God and serve Him only." Later, during his ministry, his followers directed their worship toward him, and he accepted it without a protest. In fact, he approved of it. One has to conclude that Jesus was either a disgusting hypocrite or saw himself as worthy to receive that which was reserved for God alone. On another occasion Jesus was receiving praise, and justified it by basing it on an Old Testament Psalm which stated that God had prepared such praise for Himself.[23]

Authority over Demonic Spirit Beings.[24] At the city of Capernaum Jesus was confronted by a demon-possessed man. Jesus rebuked the demons, "Be quiet and come out of him!" There was uncontested obedience. Who would have such authority? There are not many choices. The Jewish religious leaders realized this and on one occasion accused Jesus of casting out demons by Beelzebul, the ruler of the demons. The other choice is that he is deity. The response of the people at Capernaum was, "What is this message?" or, what does this show us about who he is? They recognized that such authority was evidence that He was more than a carpenter's son.

Claim to be Sinless, the Only Way, and a Ransom for Mankind.[25] The profile of Jesus that emerges from this sort of field trip into the historical records is often surprising to those who are skeptical. It was to me years ago when I doubted the truthfulness of the Biblical accounts. While several of the observations that I have included above are the result of more recent research, the limited knowledge I did have forced me to rethink my position about Jesus. In addition to all the rest, Jesus made several statements that, if true, make him unique. He claimed to be without sin: "Can any of you prove me guilty of sin?" He said that he was the exclusive way to God, "I am the way, and the truth, and the life; no one comes to the Father, but through me." And he stated that his life had such value as to redeem humankind to God, something no other human could do. In view of all this, it is not surprising that Jesus caused such a revolution in the lives of his disciples.

A SUMMARY OF SOME OF JESUS' ACTIONS

1. **Authority to forgive,** and to remove the temporal and eternal consequences of sin
2. Power to **raise the dead**
3. **Control over nature** by His command
4. **Accepted worship** from His followers
5. Demonstrated final **authority over demonic spirit beings**
6. Lived a **sinless life**
7. **His life was uniquely valuable** to redeem humankind

Figure 2.

Identifying the Logical Options

It is inevitable that anyone acquainted with the historical data concerning Jesus will have to face up to a decision concerning Him. Jesus, Himself, raised the critical question to those who had witnessed these evidences in person for more than two years. At a retreat near Caesarea Philippi, at the base of Mount Hermon, Jesus asked the disciples, "...who do you say that I am?"[26] Though removed in time 2000 years, the question is still extremely pertinent. What would you say? What options do we have?

Jesus is a LEGEND
This view was popularized prior to the twentieth century and took on unmerited legitimacy only because the evidence that refutes it was yet unknown. The position was reasonable when it was thought that the New Testament records were second-century writings. But with their early dating within the lifetime of the eyewitnesses, this view is no longer tenable.

Jesus is a LIAR

Jesus claimed to be God. A logical examination of this claim could lead to three additional options concerning him. First, either **he is** or **he is not** who he claims to be. Surveys continue to indicate that more than 90% of the people in this country believe there is a God. But if they were asked if Jesus is that God exclusively, many are skeptical. It is common to hold the opinion that Jesus is a wonderful man, a great moral teacher. But is this position logical in view of His claim to be God?

If Jesus claimed to be God and He is not who He claimed to be, then either **He knew it** or **He didn't know it.** Now if He claimed to be God knowing that He wasn't, then He is a LIAR. He lied about Himself, and received worship as if He were God Almighty. If Jesus is a liar, then He has deceived more people than any other human. He could not be the greatest liar who ever lived, and also be a great moral teacher. Besides, He would be a fool, because He died for that lie. Was Jesus a liar? His character throughout the historical accounts support a person of virtue and integrity. It is inconceivable that Jesus could sustain a committed following on such flimsy fabrication.

Jesus is a LUNATIC

At first glance, the other option seemed more plausible, i.e., he didn't know it. Jesus claimed to be God, was not, but really thought that he was. Could Jesus have been deluded? O. Quentin Hyder, practicing psychiatrist in New York City, analyzed the records of Jesus' behavior, personality and relationships for symptoms of psychiatric disorders. He concluded his study by pointing out that the evidence does not support the view that Jesus was a lunatic.

A person is free to maintain that Jesus, out of honest delusion, made His claim to deity. But if one takes this position, he does so without any psychological evidence in its support and, indeed, in spite of considerable evidence to the contrary.[27]

Jesus is the LORD

Only one option remained. Jesus claimed to be God — and he is. He is the LORD. It seems hard to imagine, but one final consideration carries a lot of weight.

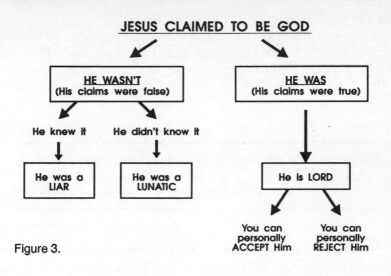

Figure 3.

The Critical Evidence: Jesus' Resurrection

Jesus promised several times during his three and one-half year ministry that he would rise from the dead.[28] Indeed, when asked by the Jews what evidence he would give to authenticate himself he said, "Destroy this temple, and in three days I will raise it up."[29] He was, in fact, speaking of his own body, i.e., the resurrection. This would be the central test to determine if he was authentic. It should be noted that *all* other founders of world religions, Buddha, Mohammed, etc. died and their relics are venerated. No other authority known to man has ever risen from the dead. I don't believe it is possible to imagine any greater credential to authenticate Jesus' claim to be deity than his resurrection. But did it really happen? Lord Darling, former Chief Justice of England and obviously trained to sift through the evidence, was satisfied that the resurrection was reasonably supported:

> The crux of the problem of whether Jesus was, or was not, what he proclaimed himself to be, must surely depend upon the truth or otherwise of the resurrection. On that greatest point we are not merely asked to have faith. In its favour as a living truth there exists such overwhelming evidence, positive and negative, factual and circumstantial, that no intelligent jury in the world could fail to bring in a verdict that the resurrection story is true.[30]

The Empty Tomb

Even the disciples themselves were skeptical. They described the women's testimony that they had seen the resurrected Jesus as "sheer imagination." And Thomas said in effect that unless he saw the physical evidence, he would never believe it.[31]

Concerning the resurrection of Jesus: a "conjuring trick with bones."

David Jenkins, Anglican bishop

Jewish sources, who were in the best position to know, never attempted to refute the empty tomb, only explain why it was empty.[32] Dr. Paul Maier, historian at Western Michigan University, sums up the current situation:

Accordingly, if all the evidence is weighed carefully and fairly, it is indeed justifiable, according to the canons of historical research, to conclude that the tomb of Joseph of Arimathea, in which Jesus was buried, was actually empty on the morning of the first Easter. And no shred of evidence has yet been discovered in literary sources, epigraphy, or archaeology that would disprove this statement.[33]

The Appearances of Jesus

The historical records indicate that subsequent to his death, Jesus "appeared to Cephas [Peter], then to the twelve. After that he appeared to more than five hundred brethren at one time, most of whom remain until now, but some have fallen asleep..."[34] C.H. Dodd has commented that "There can hardly be any purpose in mentioning the fact that most of the five hundred are still alive, unless Paul is saying, in effect, 'the witnesses are there to be questioned.'"[35] Besides appearances to his disciples, there was a convincing appearance to a brother who had before rejected him, and another that converted an enemy, Saul of Tarsus.[36]

The Transformation of the Disciples

It is a well-known fact that the disciples of Jesus abandoned and denied association with him during his arrest, trial and crucifixion.[37] The reason was fear for their own lives. Subsequently, the disciples had real experiences that they believed were literal appearances of the risen Jesus. They were transformed from scared men hiding in the Upper Room to bold proclaimers of His resurrection, even being willing to die for their conviction. Indeed, all but one of the eleven apostles died a martyr's death, yet none ever denied seeing Jesus alive after His death. Gary Habermas, apologist and philospher, a specialist on Christ's resurrection, has drawn an important conclusion: "The disciples' transformation shows that they really believed that Jesus rose from the dead and disproves the fraud (stolen body) theory both because of this change and because liars do not make martyrs."[38] The Watergate affair illustrates this point. Sophisticated lawyers, faced with the threat of a few years in prison, were unable and unwilling to maintain their fraudulent cover-up.

Make no mistake: if He rose at all
  it was His body;
if the cells dissolution did not reverse, the molecules
  reknit, the amino acids rekindle,
the Church will fall . . .
              John Updike, *Seven Stanzas at Easter*

J.N.D. Anderson, former director of the Institute of Advanced Legal Studies at the University of London, rightly said that the resurrection is "either the supreme fact in history or it is a gigantic hoax..." and if it is true, then "to fail to adjust one's life to its implications means irreparable loss."[39]

A Highly Probable Verdict

The reader must be the judge of the evidence. Is it reasonable to consider Jesus as a liar, a lunatic, or only a wonderful moral teacher. C.S. Lewis did not think so:

I am trying here to prevent anyone saying the really foolish thing that people often say about Him: "I'm ready to accept Jesus as a great moral teacher, but I don't accept His claim to be God." That is the one thing we must not say. A man who was merely a man and said the sort of things Jesus said would not be a great moral teacher. He would either be a lunatic—on a level with a man who says he is a poached egg—or else he would be the Devil of Hell. You must make your choice. Either this man was, and is, the Son of God: or else a madman or something worse. You can shut Him up for a fool, you can spit at Him and kill Him as a demon: or you can fall at His feet and call Him Lord and God. But let us not come with any patronizing nonsense about His being a great human teacher. He has not left that open to us. He did not intend to.[40]

Our imaginary field trip through the gospel accounts, though far from exhaustive, did examine much of the available historical data. As much as anything from ancient times can be, I believe the evidence validates the hypothesis that Jesus is the incarnation of the infinite-personal God.

"But the intellectual case for Christianity became powerful to me after reading Mere Christianity. At the end of the week I could not imagine how you could not believe in Jesus Christ."
Charles Colson, Chairman of Prison Fellowship

The implications of this truth have the potential of significantly changing our view of life. The issues are more than academic, they are moral. You are faced with the decision to accept or reject Him as your personal Lord. You have the freedom to turn away. But the stakes are too high to take the matter lightly. Jesus said,

I am the resurrection and the life; he who believes in Me shall live even if he dies, and everyone who lives and believes in Me shall never die. Do you believe this?

FOCUS & DISCUSSION

1. Why is it so significant to Christianity whether or not Jesus was God?

2. How significant to His identity is it that Jesus had authority over demons, death, sickness, nature, the consequences of sin, etc.? How is Jesus different than the prophets of the Old Testament through whom God performed miracles?

3. Do you think there are other logical options to explain the evidence concerning Jesus than the three indicated in this chapter (liar, lunatic, Lord)? Defend your answer with reasons.

4. What changed the minds of Jesus' contemporaries, even of many skeptics, from unbelief to faith that Jesus was God? (See Thomas - John 20:24-28; Saul- Acts 9:1-6) What does this suggest about the nature of faith?

FOUR

CAN FAITH BE REASONABLE?

Identifying the Biblical Principles

"My biggest problem had always been the intellectual reservations. I knew there was a God, but I could never see how man could have a personal relationship with Him.
Charles Colson, former special counsel
to President Richard Nixon

"What we do with what we know is what Christian knowing is all about."
Os Guinness, author

*R*ecently I was talking with a woman who was seriously considering a faith decision to follow Jesus. I will never forget her reason for hesitation. It had little to do with the intellectual concerns of purpose in life, historical reliability of the Bible, or the deity of Jesus. On those issues she had been satisfied. Instead, her hesitation was really a fear, "Will it make me into a goon!"

Contemporary Stereotypes of Faith

The misunderstandings of religious faith run deep in our society. A middleschool teacher asked one of the young students, "What do you think faith is?" By rote, the answer was given, "That's believing what you know isn't true!" When a university student was asked the same question, he said that "Faith is believing what you cannot know."

That is not an uncommon idea of faith—as though faith is a second or third best way of operating in life. Knowledge, by which is meant intellectual apprehension, is assumed to be the best way. If one cannot know, then the next best thing is just to believe anyway. The implication being that such a position is at best precarious, if not actually being stupid (a "goon").

Sometimes religious people earn labels such as anti-intellectual or a crutch for the weak. A religious group in Arkansas made national news when their alleged faith got them into trouble with the law. Claiming to have received a vision from Jesus Christ that he was returning to the earth very soon, in faith they quit their jobs, kept their children home from school, and waited. Eventually they lost their homes because they could not pay the mortgage. Social welfare officials placed their children in foster homes and back in school. The parents made a caricature of faith on the evening news in homes across America.

More recently, national news focused on a court case where parents were being tried for the death of their daughter. Of what crime were they allegedly guilty? They had "faith" that God was going to heal their daughter. Therefore, they refused any medical care for her. She died.

Can faith be reasonable? Most negative impressions of faith are generated in us by what we see in other people, such as the much-publicized Jim and Tammy Baker fiasco. But such impressions may also be generated by the eccentric neighbor next door, a religious and strange aunt, etc. Interestingly, none of these stereotypes are derived from a careful study of the Bible itself. We don't want a concept of faith derived from someone's bad example. Rather, we want to know the meaning of faith straight from the source. Therefore, we will study the Bible to identify the principles of faith. Only then can we know if faith is intended to be reasonable.

Biblical Principles of Faith

The Essential Components

Sometimes there is confusion about the word "faith." Recently I asked some people to identify differences that may exist between "faith" and "believe." Several explained distinctions with considerable confidence. Yet, the fact is that "faith" is the noun and "believe" the verb form of the same Greek word. They are interchangeable as illustrated in the familiar John 3:16: "For God so loved the world that he gave his one and only Son, that whoever believes [has faith] in him shall not perish but have eternal life." There is no difference in meaning if the words in brackets are used in place of "believes." A close synonym that may also be substituted is "trust."

1. KNOWLEDGE

The university student who said that, "Faith is believing what you cannot know," would have quite a different impression if "trust" were substituted for "faith." Let me illustrate. "Do you trust ___?", I ask, and name a person with whom he was unfamiliar. He would likely respond, "How can I trust him since I don't even know him!" "But," I would remind the student, "you said that 'Faith (trust) is believing what you cannot know.' Now you say that you cannot trust (have faith) in someone if you do not know them. Which is correct?"

The apostle Paul leaves little doubt which one he thinks is correct. Writing to the people at Rome, he communicates an interesting and logical sequence.

Figure 1.

5) Everyone who calls on the name of the Lord will be *saved*.

4) How, then, can they call on the one they have not *believed* in?

3) And how can they believe in the one of whom they have not *heard*?

2) And how can they hear without someone *preaching* to them?

1) And how can they preach unless they are *sent*?[1]

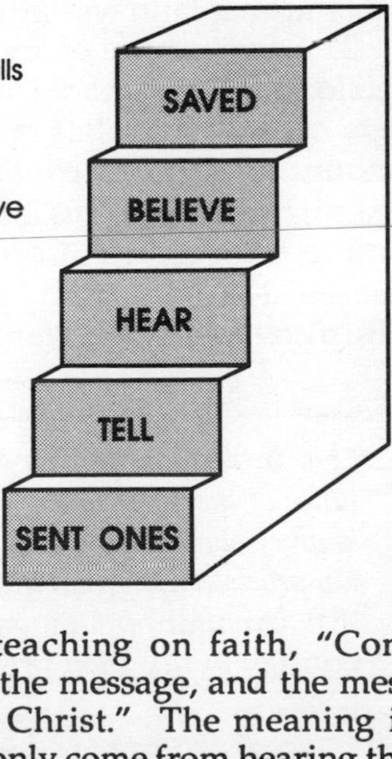

SAVED

BELIEVE

HEAR

TELL

SENT ONES

The apostle summarizes his teaching on faith, "Consequently, faith comes from hearing the message, and the message is heard through the word of Christ." The meaning is better stated as, "Belief, you see, can only come from hearing the message, and the message is the Word of [concerning] Christ."[2]

According to the apostle, faith cannot even get started without knowledge. I don't believe in 'nothing,' I believe in 'something.' Faith requires an object.

Faith is not the same as sincerity, nor does sincerity make faith genuine. Suppose that I was asked if I believed a certain chair could hold me. Since other people were sitting on similar chairs, and because the chair looked perfectly normal, I was confident that it would. Being impatient with further questioning on the matter, I exclaim emphatically, "I have no doubt in my mind the chair will hold me!" However, if someone slipped in earlier and cut the legs through so that the least touch would topple it, my confidence and sincerity would be of no avail. My faith is only as good as the object in which I place it. If the chair is good, my faith will be good. But if the chair is bad, no matter how sincere I am, I am destined for a fall.

A tragic incident at a local hospital was reported recently in the media. A nurse connected a patient to an "oxygen" source, and he immediately died. The source was mislabeled. It was actually a poisonous gas. Was the nurse competent and sincere? Did she really believe the gas was oxygen? Yes, on every count. But she was sincerely wrong. The object of her faith was defective, thus her faith was in vain.

The significance of knowledge to a valid faith must be understood. The object of Christian faith is the person of Jesus. If he is not who he claims to be, the incarnate Son of God, then no amount of sincerity, confidence, and religious experience can make it legitimate. This is precisely the conclusion of the apostle Paul to the people at Corinth. He said that "if Christ has not been raised [from the dead], then our preaching is vain, your faith also is vain...your faith is worthless."[3]

"No intelligent person desires to substitute prudent acceptance of the demonstrable for faith; but when I am told that it is precisely its immunity from proof which secures the Christian proclamation from the charge of being mythological, I reply that immunity from proof can 'secure' nothing whatever except immunity from proof, and call nonsense by its proper name."

J.S. Bezzant, English theologian

This is why it is so critical to us to know if the New Testament is an authentic and historically reliable source concerning Him. Without eyewitness testimony it would not be possible objectively to determine if Jesus was credible in his claims, thereby a worthy object of faith.

The apostle Paul is right. I can only put faith in Jesus if I know about Him. And only if that knowledge indicates reasonable certainty of his deity will my faith in him be any good. I cannot even get started into the area of personal faith without using my mind and interacting with the evidence. This first component of faith as taught in the Bible is certainly more attractive than the anti-intellectual caricature of it that I had as a college student.

2. WILL

A story is told of a stunt man capable of walking a tight-wire across the expanse of Niagara Falls. On one occasion he accomplished the amazing feat pushing a wheelbarrow. Promoters of the event asked the cheering crowd how many believed that he could do it again. The crowd roared affirmatively. He then asked for a volunteer to ride in the wheelbarrow! No one came forward.

Knowledge is one thing, but choosing to commit one's life to that knowledge is another matter. Likewise, knowledge of Jesus is indispensable to faith, but it is only the first component. I could know exhaustively the evidence supporting the life of Jesus, and have no faith at all. The second faith component involves our will. This is illustrated once again in Paul's letter to the people at Rome.

> But not all the Israelites accepted the good news. For Isaiah says, "Lord, who has believed our message?"...But I ask: Did they not hear? Of course they did... Again I ask, Did Israel not understand?... But concerning Israel he [God] says, "All day long I have held out my hands to a disobedient and obstinate people."[4]

The people of Israel had disobeyed God, i.e., they lacked faith. Paul is questioning why that was so. He asks the question whether they knew what God wanted. If not, the reason for their lack of faith would be a lack of knowledge.

I had a similar experience with my sons. Upon leaving my home for the day, I gave instructions for them to mow the lawn.

When I returned that evening I noted that either the grass grew at an unprecedented rate in a few hours or they had failed to do what I had asked. I strongly suspected the latter. I went to them and used a question familiar to every parent, "Didn't you hear me?" Did I really think that at the moment I had spoken my instructions to them that morning, the physics of sound waves had failed? No, I was quite confident my voice had reached their ears, but I was giving them the benefit of the doubt with my question. It turned out they did not have a knowledge problem. They had a "will" problem — they didn't want to mow the lawn.

In the text above, Paul uses the same approach. He also concludes that the Israelites' problem was not caused by a lack of knowledge, but due to disobedience and obstinance, i.e., a "will" problem.

Several years ago my wife and I had a disagreement (the most recent I can recall [sic]). I no longer remember the issue, but it occurred on a Sunday afternoon. I was right, and she was wrong, but she wouldn't admit it! About the time we were getting quite intense, the doorbell rang. I went to the door and was "thrilled" to see some friends from another city who had stopped by because they were in the area. The transformation that took place in my wife and me at that moment would make metamorphosis from a worm to a butterfly pale in comparison! We were instantly congenial and pleasant. After our friends left, I reflected on what happened. What was it that changed us? The doorbell?

I was not that naive. The doorbell did not change us — *we* did. By a deliberate choice, an act of my will, I changed. Why didn't I change sooner? I certainly knew from seminars, books, and experience that my obstinate behavior was inappropriate to maintain harmony in a marriage relationship. The reason I didn't change before the doorbell rang, though, was that I did not want to! I was exercising my will.

Faith is like that. In spite of the knowledge concerning Jesus that we have gained, if we do not exercise our wills, we have all the faith we are ever going to have — none. Unless we make a choice concerning who Jesus is, there will be no faith. A consenting will is the second essential component of the Bible's definition of faith. And that is certainly more attractive than the caricature of faith as emotion that I had rejected years earlier.

3. RESPONSE

Faith is knowing the truth about Jesus, and being willing to accept him. But one of Jesus' parables (Matthew 21:28-32) identifies another factor in faith: Faith is not good intentions.

> "What do you think? There was a man who had two sons, He went to the first and said, 'Son, go and work today in the vineyard.' 'I will not,' he answered, but later he changed his mind and went. Then the father went to the other son and said the same thing. He answered, 'I will, sir,' but he did not go. Which of the two did what his father wanted?" "The first," they answered. Jesus said to them, "I tell you the truth, the tax collectors and the prostitutes are entering the kingdom of God ahead of you. For John came to you to show you the way of righteousness, and you did not believe him, but the tax collectors and the prostitutes did. And even after you saw this, you did not repent and believe him."[5]

The point of Jesus is that faith is proven by its action. If there is no response derived from the will and the knowledge, then there is no faith either. In other words, according to the teaching of the Bible, to qualify as legitimate, faith must consist of all three components: knowledge, will and response. Frequently, I talk with people who consider abandoning any further pursuit of truth once they are satisfied intellectually, and are no longer inclined negatively toward it. They want to walk away. But, response is concerned with the implications of the truth for my life. The apostle James is quite concerned with this third component of faith when he says that "faith by itself, if it is not accompanied by action, is dead."[6]

The three corners of a triangle can be used to represent the three essential components of Biblical faith. Based on this dia-

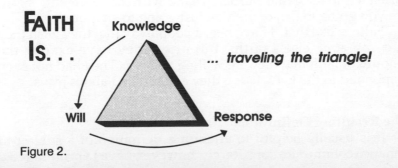

FAITH IS. . . Knowledge   ... *traveling the triangle!*

Will   Response

Figure 2.

gram, faith is traveling the triangle. Jesus spoke a parable il-
lustrating that there are really only two types of people; that is,
those who travel the triangle and those who don't. The consequences in their lives are amazingly different:

> "And why do you call Me, 'Lord, Lord,' and do not do what
> I say? Everyone who comes to Me, and *hears* My words, and
> *acts* upon them, I will show you whom he is like; he is like a
> man building a house, who dug deep and laid a foundation
> upon the rock; and when a flood arose, the river burst
> against that house and could not shake it, because it had
> been well built. But the one who *has heard*, and *has not acted*
> *accordingly*, is like a man who built a house upon the ground
> without any foundation; and the river burst against it and
> immediately it collapsed, and the ruin of that house was
> great." [emphasis added][7]

The story is told of a fisherman with an enviable reputation
— he always caught a large quantity of fish. But he also always
fished alone. An elderly gentleman from a distant city, saying
that he wanted to learn fishing as a retirement hobby, begged the
fisherman to teach him the sport. He refused repeatedly but the
persistent doggedness of the retiree finally broke him down. At
the lake the elderly man was surprised that the great fisherman
had only a metal box and a net for gear. Upon reaching a remote
corner of the lake and leaving the motor running, the fisherman
opened his metal box, pulled out some dynamite sticks, lit them,
heaved them overboard and raced the other way with the boat.
After the blast, he circled around and began netting the fish that
had been stunned. The senior citizen had seen enough of this
fishing method. He pulled his game warden badge from his
pocket and flashed it before the fisherman. With but a momen-
tary pause, the fisherman pulled out more dynamite, lit and
thrust it into the game warden's hand with the comment, "Now,
are you going to fish or are you just going to sit there!"
   Faith is like that. I have heard people say that they wish they
had someone else's faith. But often they have exactly the
amount of faith that they are willing to have. They had not even
responded to the knowledge they already had about Jesus.

The Resulting Definitions
   It is usually helpful to attempt a definition of a subject to
enhance communication. Rarely, however, have I encountered a

definition of faith. Faith is easier to illustrate than define, but I have created two that have helped me.

Head to Foot Commitment
The first is a homely one that derives from a brief anatomy lesson (I always assume that every one's favorite subject in school was biology!). If we were asked to parallel the appropriate anatomical parts with the three points of the faith triangle, the head (=knowledge), the heart (=will), and the feet (=response) would be our likely choices. Consequently, we may define faith as **"making a commitment to God from head to foot."** At least it is simple! But had I heard such a definition when I was questioning everything in college, I would either have denied it as true or I would have had to rethink my caricatures.

I would never have imagined faith starting with the head, i.e., with reason, evidence and knowledge. This definition says that once the mind is satisfied, the process, figuratively speaking, moves to the heart where the will must interact with the data concerning Jesus. I imagined that people of faith were "no-minds" who acted on the basis of emotion alone. Finally, the definition, again figuratively, moves the process to the feet or place where there is life response. The whole person is satisfied, and a new alignment or orientation to Jesus is established.

A Decision-Making Process
The second definition is more descriptive: **Faith is a decision-making process, based upon the Word of God, and without regard to the emotional questioning of that Word.**
...*A Decision-making Process*. I find it helpful to apply the definition to starting a new business — a fast-food restaurant. I would want to begin with some market research on the eating preferences of people in the area, the number of competing businesses already operating, availability of a building site, etc. The gathering of this critical information is equivalent to the "knowledge" component of the faith triangle. But I do not have a restaurant even if I have the most complete market research ever done. Eventually my interaction with the information must result in a decision whether or not to build. Even if my decision is affirmative, I still do not have a business. The knowledge and decision must be followed up with building, contracting with suppliers, hiring, and a variety of other responses that are consistent with the former two components. The deci-

sion-making process that I have just described is analogous to traveling the faith triangle. I study the person of Jesus, make a decision concerning him, and then follow him in obedience.

"Hell is God's great compliment to the reality of human freedom and the dignity of human choice."
                                        G.K. Chesterton, British writer

---

...*Based upon the Word of God*. However, the definition does not stop there. It has two conditions to guide the decision-making process. First, the source is to be the Word of God that we have analyzed for reliability in chapter two. It may also include evidence about Jesus discussed in chapter three. Finally, in the sense that the Word of God is seen as the truth of God, we may even include evidences in the natural world such as order, design, purpose, personality, etc. This is certainly superior to ignorance, prejudice, and deception that shaped my earlier beliefs.

...*Without Regard to the Emotional Questioning of that Word*. The second condition recognizes human emotion as a reality, but denies it should determine the outcome of the decision-making process of faith. Emotions are not always consistent with what is right — jealousy, lust, depression, insecurity — being obvious examples. Furthermore, a faith decision to follow Jesus may run counter to emotions linked to peer pressure, popularity, and pride. Therefore, it is better that emotions add an in-depth, whole person experience, but within the context defined by the decision-making process.

The Premier Example: Abraham

An incident in the life of Abraham will help to illustrate this definition of faith. Isaac was a miracle child for Abraham and Sarah. Born when they were very old, he was a child through whom God promised to give them descendents "as the stars of the heavens" and "as the sand which is on the sea shore," and through whom "all the nations of the earth shall be blessed."[8] Isaac, born so late in his parent's lives, their only child, and the subject of such marvelous promises, was very dear to Abraham and Sarah.

Then the day came when God tested Abraham's faith: "Take now your son, your only son, whom you love, Isaac, and go to the land of Moriah; and offer him there as a burnt offering on one of the mountains of which I will tell you." The thought is repulsive, but this event prefigured another one that would be the single, most important event in the history of humankind.

I could think of a lot of reasons to sleep in the next morning after hearing a message like that. But Abraham rose early to go — I suppose because he felt so good about it! No, but he chose (will) to be obedient (response) to the Word of God he had received (knowledge). The emotional questioning that undoubtedly flooded through him did not determine his response. But struggle he did. How could God fulfill the many promises that he made concerning Isaac if Isaac were dead? He knew that God could not be unfaithful. By the time that he arrived at the place of sacrifice three days later, he had resolved it in his mind: "Abraham reasoned that God could raise the dead..."[9]

As the altar was prepared on the mountain, Isaac asked a pertinent question, "...where is the lamb for the burnt offering?" Abraham hoped against hope when he said that "God himself will provide the lamb for the burnt offering, my son." Not until he raised the knife to slay his son did God cry out, "Do not lay a hand on the boy...Now I know that you fear God, because you have not withheld from me your son, your only son." I'm sure that Abraham did not debate with God whether He was certain that He didn't want Isaac to die! With great rejoicing that his son could live, he substituted a ram caught by its horns in a thicket. God *did* provide the lamb for the sacrifice. Abraham gave that place a name, "The Lord Will Provide."

It is natural to focus on the intense human elements of this event, while knowing nothing of its greater significance. Most would think that the event has no relevance for our lives today, but that is a serious oversight. The "land of Moriah" where this event took place about 2000 B.C., is the area of Judea around Jerusalem. It is later called Mount Moriah, and is the hill on which the Jewish temple was later built.[10] That was also the hill of Golgotha where Jesus died — the hill that Abraham 2000 years earlier had named, "The Lord Will Provide." When Jesus first began his public ministry, he was introduced by John the Baptist as "the Lamb of God, who takes away the sin of the world!"[11] He died so that the children of Abraham could live, i.e., "to those who are of the faith of Abraham." The lamb that spared Abraham's son physically, foreshadowed the Lamb that

God provided 2000 years later on the same hillside so that
Abraham's descendents by faith could live spiritually and eternally.

> Consider Abraham: "He believed God, and it was credited
> to him as righteousness." Understand, then, that those who
> believe are children of Abraham. The Scripture foresaw that
> God would justify the Gentiles by faith, and announced the
> gospel in advance to Abraham: "All nations will be blessed
> through you." So those who have faith are blessed along
> with Abraham, the man of faith.[12]
> Therefore, the promise comes...by grace...for us who believe
> in him who raised Jesus our Lord from the dead. He was
> delivered over to death for our sins and was raised to life for
> our salvation.[13]

It is hard to imagine that this is all just coincidence. The
"seed" [singular] of Abraham, i.e., Jesus Christ, has made
possible spiritual descendents who number as the stars and
sandgrains, a blessing to every nation on the earth.

Life-Changing Dimensions of Faith

Even if I had known about the three components and the
definitions of faith (the Biblical principles) during my search for
answers as a young man, I don't think I would have responded
to it. It would have helped remove some of the vagueness of the
concept that was in my mind. But there was still a big question
mark about faith that bothered me a lot — I wasn't sure that I
would be able to keep it up. At that time I viewed being a Christian as following a set of impossible rules. I despised hy-
pocrites, and I didn't want to be one. Later I realized that my
concern stemmed from a critical misunderstanding of how a
person becomes a Christian.

A New Relationship: The GIFT of God's Presence

I viewed faith as a human enterprise — choosing a set of
spiritual guidelines to follow. The focus was on how well I
might be able to match my life to the rules. The day came when
I discovered that faith was a relationship — with God. Since
that time my study and experience have confirmed that truth.

The discussion that follows is the way that I would explain the life-changing dimensions of faith today.

Jesus, at the autumn Feast of Tabernacles in Jerusalem, focused attention on this matter:

"On the last and greatest day of the Feast, Jesus stood and said in a loud voice. 'If anyone is thirsty, let him come to me and drink. Whoever believes in me, as the Scripture has said, streams of living water will flow from within him.' By this he meant the Spirit whom those who believed in him were later to receive."[14]

It is obvious that Jesus was referring to something supernatural — the Spirit of God within a person. How could this be? The naturalistic presuppositions of my scientific training had caused me to view such an idea with incredulity. But there is no mistaking the teaching. The night before his crucifixion, Jesus told his disciples that after he ascended they would receive *another* Counselor, the Spirit of truth, who "will be in you."[15] The apostle Paul affirms this, too: "Do you not know that your body is a temple of the Holy Spirit, who is in you, whom you have received from God?"[16]

How and when does this happen? Paul explains in his letter to the Ephesian believers: "And you also were included in Christ when you heard the word of truth, the gospel of your salvation. Having believed, you were marked in him with a seal, the promised Holy Spirit, who is a deposit guaranteeing our inheritance..."[17] The "seal" is a mark of authenticity — that the believer is really a member of the family of God. The "deposit" is an earnest signifying that God will never abandon his followers in this life, and assures fulfillment of his promise to give them eternal life after death.

This adds a relational dimension to the faith triangle. When we travel the triangle, thereby trusting in Jesus Christ as the object of faith, we receive the divine person of the Holy Spirit to live within us. The teaching that the Christian faith is not just a moral code to live by is indispensable to one's understanding of its dynamic nature.

That is why Jesus was so direct when he spoke to Nicodemus, a representative of the very religious Pharisaic party.[18] Nicodemus lived by a high ethic, a moral man. But Jesus told him he was not going to heaven ("enter the kingdom") on that basis alone. Rather, he must be "born of the Spirit." Literally, the expression "born again" means to be given new life from above. Many people that I talk to think that they will go to heaven because they have cleaned up their act or have gone straight. It is something they can pull off if they try hard enough. But not so. Jesus said we become Christians when God does a miracle of spiritual conception within us as we respond in faith to him. The result is a faith in which we experience the gift of God's presence changing us within instead of one that controls us by an external code of do's and dont's.

A New Freedom: The GIFT of God's Grace

So, as a young person, I had misunderstood the nature of the Christian faith. I now know it is not so much a religion as it is a relationship. Some reflection upon Jesus will help us to see why. Christians do not think of themselves as following the *teachings* of Jesus, but rather Jesus *Himself*. The reason is simple — Jesus is alive. You can find disciples of Muhammad or Gandhi but only in the sense that they try to live by the teachings these leaders left behind. Muhammad and Gandhi are dead. Their followers cannot have a personal relationship with them. In contrast, a Christian's faith is a relationship with the person of Jesus Christ who is very much alive, and whom he/she fully expects to see face to face.

"It is not a mere acceptance of certain beliefs and dogmas, though they are necessary, but essentially it is living in close fellowship with Christ. It is not only a religion to be practiced, but also a life to be lived."
Bishop John A. Subhan (convert from Islam)

This insight helps to erase a frequent misunderstanding, i.e., how to get and sustain faith. Some may understand me to be saying that faith is, first, exercising their will to affirm Jesus, and then, second, exerting a little discipline to order their lives according to his teachings. That is what people think who never have looked seriously at what Jesus has to say. His example and teachings are relentless: "...love your enemies..."; "...every one who looks on a woman to lust for her has committed adultery with her already in his heart..."; "...no one of you can be my disciple who does not give up all his own possessions..."; forgive one another "seventy times seven" times; "...you are to be perfect..."! After a few weeks or months of clenched fists and teeth gritted in sheer determination, a person will become exasperated. Bertrand Russell, British mathematician and philosopher, once said, "Love your enemies is good advice, but too difficult for us." Trying to live like Jesus is not just difficult — it is impossible. Until we are shaken by the experience of our own moral ineptness, we will not appreciate the need for the gift of God's grace in our lives. We will also resist Jesus' analysis of our condition.

> He [Jesus] went on: "What comes out of a man is what makes him 'unclean.' For from within, out of men's hearts, come evil thoughts, sexual immorality, theft, murder, adultery, greed, malice, deceit, lewdness, envy, slander, arrogance and folly. All these evils come from inside and make a man 'unclean.'"[19]

In the privacy of our own hearts and minds, we all know that what He said is true. As the British writer, G.K. Chesterton, has said: "The one doctrine of Christianity which is empirically verifiable is the fallenness of man." Some may deny it, but our experience of trying to be really good only serves to remind us of the need for grace, i.e., unmerited favor. The apostle Paul explains: "For it is by grace you have been saved, through faith — and this not from yourselves, it is the gift of God — not by works, so that no one can boast."[20] Grace was necessary because we are morally inadequate before a holy God: "There is none righteous, not even one...no one who seeks God." In fact, if you have an interest in God and are attracted to faith, it is not your own doing, for Jesus said that "No one can come to me unless the Father who sent me draws him."[21] One biblical passage in particular says all this quite clearly:

> But when the kindness and love of God our Savior appeared, he saved us, not because of righteous things we had done, but because of his mercy. He saved us through the washing of rebirth and renewal by the Holy Spirit...so that, having been justified by his grace, we might become heirs having the hope of eternal life.[22]

In view of these life-changing dimensions, the triangle is no longer an adequate figure to represent faith. The components are right, but we lack the desire and the power to do it. But what if the Holy Spirit Himself is placed as a fourth point at the center to create a supernatural third dimension? For us even to be open to the evidence concerning the Bible and Jesus requires the convicting activity of the Holy Spirit. If, by His prompting, we accept the gift of salvation through faith in Jesus Christ, the Holy Spirit takes up permanent residency within us. He transforms our fallen nature and desires from within, and provides the power to travel the triangle, as Paul says, "... it is God who works in you to **will** and to **act** according to his good purpose."[23]

Figure 3.

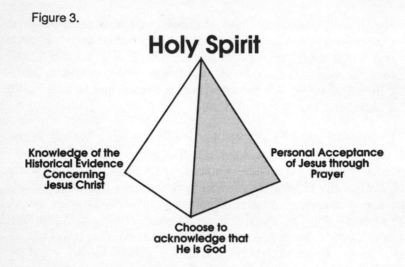

Holy Spirit

Knowledge of the
Historical Evidence
Concerning
Jesus Christ

Personal Acceptance
of Jesus through
Prayer

Choose to
acknowledge that
He is God

A New Hope: The GIFT of God's Heaven

The Christian faith promises a new relationship with the God who is really there. It also promises a new freedom from having to be good enough to earn God's approval. His grace means forgiveness, and new power and joy in life. But one preconceived fallacy about faith still remains.

I grew up thinking that no one in this life could ever know whether or not God had approved of them. That was a judgment only God could make after I died and the good and bad deeds had been tallied. I had to try as hard as I could and hope for the best.

It should now be apparent that this notion is inconsistent with the biblical principles of faith. How can one's destiny be uncertain if the object of faith, Jesus Christ, is certain? How can our deeds be the deciding factor if our relationship with God is a matter of grace? The apostle John sets the record straight:

"God has given us eternal life, and this life is in his Son, He who has the Son has life; he who does not have the Son of God does not have life. I write these things to you who believe in the name of the Son of God so that you may **know** that you have eternal life."[24]

It is clear that God has already revealed who will go to heaven. In one of the most familiar passages in the Bible, He said that "whoever believes in him [Jesus] shall not perish but have eternal life." The apostle Paul said that "the gift of God is eternal life in Christ Jesus our Lord."[25] We can know right now that there is life after death, and that we will spend it eternally in heaven with God. It all depends on what we decide about Jesus.

Testing Subjective Claims

Our testing of the God hypothesis and the Christian faith began by looking only at the objective evidence of science and history. It is now obvious that there are also some very important subjective, experiential elements as well. Sometimes I am told that these subjective , anecdotal aspects don't really prove anything. Josh McDowell answers this challenge with an illustration.

> For example, let's say a student comes into the room and says, 'Guys, I have a stewed tomato in my right tennis shoe. This tomato has changed my life. It has given me a peace and love and joy that I never experienced before...It is hard to argue with a student like that if his life backs up what he says...A personal testimony is often a subjective argument for the reality of something...There are two questions or tests I apply to a subjective experience. First, what is the objective reality for the subjective experience, and second, how many other people have had the same subjective experience from being related to the objective reality?[26]

When asked how he accounts for his life change, the student would answer, "A stewed tomato in my right tennis shoe." But to find even one other person in the entire world that has had a similar life change as a result of a stewed tomato in their right tennis shoe is improbable. The objective reality is more than a little suspect when it cannot be verified repeatedly in others.

When a Christian is asked for the objective reality that has resulted in a significant subjective life change, he/she would answer, "The person of Christ and his resurrection." How many others share this same result from a relationship with Jesus Christ? The evidence is overwhelming. There are millions of people from every nationality and profession that have experienced this kind of positive life change. Such broad confirmation greatly increases the validity of the life-changing dimensions of faith in Jesus.

Before Jesus left this earth he told his followers that he was going to prepare a place for them in heaven. He added: "And if I go and prepare a place for you, I will come back and take you to be with me that you also may be where I am."[27] According to Jesus, the time is coming when every person that has ever lived will stand before Him. There is only one issue raised on that day of accounting: What did you decide to do about Him?[28]

It will be too late then to choose your side. It is the better wisdom to deal with this issue before then — to settle out of court! Then you can have assurance that the apostle Paul had: "Therefore, there is now no condemnation for those who are in Christ Jesus...[He] set me free from...sin and death."[29]

FOCUS & DISCUSSION ─────────────────

1. In what sense can it be said that Christian faith is rational?
2. The point was made in this chapter that faith in Jesus is a matter of personal decision. What implication does this have for universalism (all people are accepted into heaven by God)?
3. How is the third principle of faith ("Response") different from the teaching that good deeds are necessary to get approval from God and earn heaven?
4. Jesus taught that those who put their faith in Him would be given the presence of the Holy Spirit within them (John 7:37-39). Why is this necessary?
5. Is becoming a Christian more of a reformation or a transformation? Which image is most appropriate to becoming a Christian: a) remodeling an old house, or b) metamorphosis of a caterpillar into a butterfly?

FIVE

WHERE AM I?

Analyzing Unbelief, Belief, And Doubt

*"I thought it was very peculiar that I had acquired everything
I had wanted as a child — wealth, fame and accomplishment
in my career, I had beautiful children and a lifestyle that
seemed terrific, and yet I was totally and miserably unhappy.
I found it very frightening that one could acquire all these
things and still be so miserable."*
  Racquel Welch, actress

*"The probability of life originating from accident is
comparable to the probability of the unabridged dictionary
resulting from an explosion in a printing factory."*
  Edwin Carlston, biologist at Princeton

*S*everal years ago my wife and I were doing a community
survey of people's views concerning Christian faith. A rather
large, robust man came to the door at one home. When I presented him with, "Would you be willing to answer some questions concerning your faith?", he nearly exploded. The tirade
that followed, accompanied by anger, red face, and bulging
eyes, was frightening. Fortunately, my wife was there and I
managed to hide behind her through most of it! Not wanting to
leave on a sour note, we changed the subject to compliment him
on his manicured lawn and beautiful flower beds. We hit a positive nerve. Being a yardsman myself, we engaged in a lively exchange of ideas and strategies. Before we left his home, I
wanted to find out how to avoid a repeat performance of this
encounter at the next house we visited. Had we done something to cause his ire?

He told us his story. At a previous residence he had lived alone except for a very special pet dog. He also had what he called a religious neighbor. On one occasion he let his pet dog out in the morning and was watching through the window. About the time the little dog was doing to the neighbor's shrubbery what dogs do to shrubbery, the neighbor stepped out of the bushes where he had been hiding and kicked the little dog nearly to the street. (Undoubtedly there was the religious neighbor's side of the story—which I was not hearing). Because of internal injuries, the little dog had to be put to sleep. By this time the man is again red in the face and blurted out, "Now if that is what faith is like, I don't want any part of it!"

My first estimate of this man was that he was clearly a rabid unbeliever. After hearing his story, I knew that it was not that simple.

The Analysis of Unbelief and Doubt

Could such unbelief as this man manifested be justified by the circumstances? Is this man's unbelief different from that of others who do not believe, but have no hostility at all? Where do the familiar spiritual doubts fit into the subject of faith? To have a more complete understanding of these matters, it is necessary to examine the counterparts of faith, namely, unbelief and doubt. As a result, we will be enabled to determine more specifically in which position each of us stands.

Its Nature

I have asked many groups of people to tell me what comes to their minds when they hear the word "unbelief." Typically, they produce the following one-word descriptions:

doubt	unsure	blind	rejection
unknowing	decision	wavering	rebellion
distrust	ignorance	indecision	arrogant
skepticism	willful	hard-hearted	

Even a casual examination of these words suggests that they do not represent a single concept. Indeed, there is quite a difference between "ignorance" and "rejection", and between "wavering" and "rebellion." Are these diverse descriptions the result of surveying confused people, or are they honest attempts to communicate a complex subject?

Imagine with me that a lost tribe has just been discovered in the jungles of the Amazon. I volunteer to go to them so that I can share the historical facts concerning Jesus. Assuming language compatibility, our dialogue makes me acutely aware of the consequences of their years of isolation. They have never heard of any events of human civilization, much less the details about Jesus. They are in unbelief concerning him; that is, they lack faith in Jesus. In this case there is a special reason for their unbelief — ignorance. Remember: How can they believe in what they have never heard? Knowledge is the first component necessary for faith. They do not know about Jesus, the object of Christian faith. Let us identify their condition as **ignorant unbelief**.

Now I spend every day, for several months, tirelessly telling these people about the basis for purpose and meaning, the historical and scientific evidence for the biblical writings, and what Jesus had said and done. After each session the people question and debate. Some are persuaded by a point or two, but wonder about others. They are back and forth over the issues, unable to establish a firm position concerning Jesus. They are still in unbelief, but for a different reason: they can't decide. The second component necessary for faith is an affirming will. They will need to make a choice about Jesus. Let us label their new condition as **doubt**.

Finally, after an additional period of teaching and questioning, the chief stands up to render his decision. To my horror it is now revealed that they are a cannibal tribe — there is a lot at stake here! The chief suggests to the others that I am "out to lunch." They reject the message concerning Jesus. They are in unbelief, but for a third reason: they have chosen not to believe. Let us express this condition as **decisioned unbelief**.

Its Forms

We are now able to make sense of the list of one-word descriptions of unbelief that people usually give. They identify three aspects of the complex nature of unbelief which can be categorized into the conditions through which the lost tribe progressed.

1. IGNORANCE — unknowing, blind

2. DOUBT— distrust, skepticism, unsure, wavering, indecision
3. DECISION — willful, hard-hearted, rejection, rebellion, arrogant

Unbelief exists in these three forms. The many words that come to people's minds when they think of unbelief are just synonyms of the basic three forms. The relationship between the forms is clarified by the diagram in Figure 1.

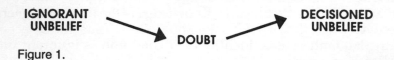

IGNORANT UNBELIEF → **DOUBT** → **DECISIONED UNBELIEF**

Figure 1.

The simplicity of determining the position we are in with regard to Jesus Christ should be apparent. I recall the time in my own life when I could no longer say that I didn't know enough about Jesus — that I was ignorant of the facts. Interestingly, in my own mind, I had not decided to reject him either. Or had I? My first exposure to the evidences for the Bible and faith had left me unsure and wavering, i.e., in doubt. I went through a necessary time of discrimination and hesitation before a firm position could be taken. But additional months of fact gathering did not change my indecision. I had already been persuaded that the evidence for Jesus' deity was excellent. Yet I remained in doubt and kept thinking that I needed to read one more book, check out one more fact, and so on, *ad infinitum*. Looking back on this time from my perspective today, I believe my skepticism had become, in reality, decisioned unbelief masquerading as doubt.

Its Causes

There are two primary blocks to a reasonable biblical faith. They are ignorance and willful rejection. Why this is so is evident when we recall the faith triangle. Knowledge concerning Jesus and an affirming will are the first two essential components of faith. When ignorance replaces knowledge and rejection replaces affirmation, there can be no faith.

If I were in ignorant unbelief, how could I get out of that condition? Search for, be open to, and receive the readily-available information concerning the object of faith — Jesus. Five Christian missionary couples were in South America attempting to tell the Auca Indian tribe about Jesus. The tribe was clearly in ignorant unbelief since the missionaries had not even met them yet, or understood their language. One day, in an attempt to make personal contact, the five husbands were killed by the Aucas in a surprise attack. In spite of tremendous grief over the loss of their husbands, the wives flew over the tribe and dropped gifts from their small airplane. This act of courage, love and forgiveness, eventually won the opportunity for contact, and later, communication with the people. Ignorance concerning Jesus was removed by teaching the facts about His life. They later made a faith decision to accept Jesus as their Savior. An incredible life change took place. In fact, the chief of the tribe later baptized the son of the missionary he had personally killed.[1]

What if I were in the unbelief position of doubt concerning Jesus? How could I move from that position? I must decide how much information is enough to give relative certainty about Jesus' identity, and to say either "yes" or "no" to him as my Savior and Lord.

Finally, what would I do if I were in decisioned unbelief? There is no way out except to reconsider my position by returning to "doubt" where I reexamine the evidence to see if a "yes" to Jesus is not more reasonable and appropriate than a "no."

"Contemporary unbelief does not rest on science as it did towards the close of the last century. It denies both science and religion. It is no longer the skepticism of reason in the presence of miracle. It is a passionate unbelief."
                                        Albert Camus, French writer

---

However, sometimes it is not that clear-cut. The two causes of unbelief, that is, ignorance and unwillingness, may be interrelated. The apostle Paul, speaking of certain unbelieving people, said that "They are darkened in their understanding and separated from God because of the ignorance that is in them due to the hardening of their hearts."[2] It is disconcerting to think that if we fail to respond positively to what we know is true, a hardening of the will may take place that immunizes us, so to speak, against hearing and accepting additional truth. We have already indicated above that we are free to harden our hearts and willfully say "no" to the knowledge of Jesus that we have. Now we have to admit that our hard-heartedness may make us blind to truth by its refusal to even listen or be open to the evidence at all. Furthermore, our stubborn wills may even attempt to rationalize the rightness of such a position.

Sometimes I have wondered about the irate man that my wife and I had called upon at his home. What form of unbelief was he in? My first impression was decisioned unbelief. He appeared to be rebellious and hard-hearted. But after hearing his story, I changed my mind. I think he was in ignorant unbelief. He had rejected a caricature of faith, not the real thing. He seemed to know little about Jesus at all. The concern I had for him was whether his anger over a foolish act by his so-called religious neighbor would forever shut him off from getting the knowledge about Jesus that he needed to make a legitimate choice. Because of the stereotypes and caricatures of faith in society today, I have come to believe that ignorant unbelief, caused by a refusal to listen or be open to the evidence, is the most common form of unbelief. In fact, this is the position from which the apostle Paul said he came as a former persecutor of Christians: "...yet I was shown mercy, because I acted ignorantly in unbelief..."[3]

The Analysis of Belief

The observation that we have free will, results in the possibility of saying "no" to the truth claim of the Christian faith. But to be truly free means that we may also choose to say "yes." This is the alternative to one of the unbelief positions, i.e., belief. Figure 2 indicates the positions we may be in, and the choices we are free to make.

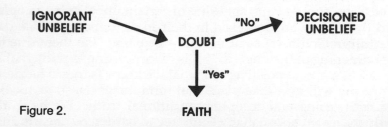

Figure 2.

Its Operation

The idea that faith necessitated a personal decision became clear enough to me during my own search for certainty about God. What I did not understand at all, though, was the way in which faith was to operate in my life. Only later have I come to recognize that there is a counterfeit of faith which masquerades as the real thing. If the counterfeit is mistaken for the genuine, our faith in God can lead to disappointment and bitterness rather than fulfillment.

The Counterfeit: Contract Faith

I grew up thinking of faith in terms of a contract. The scenario went something like this: I was to believe that Jesus was the Son of God. In return, God would provide certain benefits for me — happiness, success, wealth, and health — small things! This seemed only right in view of the sacrifice it was for me to conform my life to follow Him. And I would continue to follow God as long as He lived up to His end of my imaginary contract. If He didn't come through to meet my expectations — well, forget it! In other words, this scenario describes a faith contract with conditions written in — "I'll believe if ..."

A classic example of this approach to faith is an incident in the life of Thomas, one of Jesus' disciples. Jesus had told his followers on several occasions that He would rise from the dead.[4] When Thomas was told by eyewitnesses that it had actually happened, he responded by saying, "Unless I see the nail marks in His hands and put my finger where the nails were, and put my hand into His side, I will not believe it."[5] Eight days later Thomas fell at Jesus' feet and exclaimed, "My Lord and my God!" Jesus then said to him: "Because you have seen me you have believed; blessed are those who have not seen and yet have believed."

What was Thomas' problem? His alleged faith in Jesus was conditional — he insisted that he must physically see Jesus rather than believe the resurrection on the basis of what Jesus had promised beforehand. Thomas said, in effect, that he did not believe in Jesus because he would not trust His Word (or the eyewitnesses), but would only believe if..., and expressed his conditions.

In rescuing the nation of Israel from slavery in Egypt, God demonstrated his faithfulness by overcoming impossible odds with many miracles. He then brought them to the land of Canaan and promised that He would take them in. Twelve men were sent into the country as spies for 40 days, and returned with two reports.[6] The majority report of ten said that while the land was excellent, the inhabitants were giants and their cities were strongly fortified. Thus, the people might as well head back to Egypt because there was no way the land could be taken. What would change their minds? Perhaps if they had a dozen stealth bombers? — Or a battery of missiles? Their position was, "God, we believe you could take us in, if..." Unfortunately, this is not faith at all—it is a counterfeit.

The Genuine: Surrender Faith

Contract faith, the counterfeit, is putting the onus on God to perform. Actually, it is acting as though we were God and He must do our bidding. That is not exactly the appropriate attitude of a finite to the infinite! We are the ones in need of God, not vice versa. We must come to God on God's terms, not on ours.

Furthermore, it implies that we don't think God can back up his Word, i.e., He isn't capable. But, if faith is as good as its object, and the object of Christian faith is the incarnate God, Jesus Christ, then whatever He says is the last word on any subject. Setting conditions is assuming that God has limitations. Surrender faith is not something I have to generate emotionally, or a confidence placed in the church or government. Surrender faith is trusting unconditionally the infinitely powerful, wise, loving, and just God who created and sustains all that exists. What He says, He can and does do. If we know God that way, then the "decision-making process based on the Word of God" is a very reasonable way to live. Instead of "I'll believe if...", it is, "I believe."

The counterfeit and genuine faith mentalities are illustrated by the Israeli spies. The majority reported that, despite God's command, a successful invasion of Palestine was not possible. The minority report of the remaining two spies, Joshua and Caleb, stated that since God had instructed them to take the land, they should proceed immediately to do so. What is the difference? Joshua and Caleb were basing their recommended action on a powerful and faithful God who had promised this land to them. No conditions could outweigh this single factor. But not so with the rest of the people. By following the majority report, they were indicating that other factors were more important in their consideration than God's Word. If those factors changed, then okay. Their's was a contract with conditions, a counterfeit for faith. God's response to them underscores this point: "How long will these people treat me with contempt? How long will they refuse to believe in me, in spite of all the miraculous signs I have performed among them?"[7] The result was forty years of wilderness wanderings until Joshua and Caleb led a new generation into the promised land. The counterfeit of faith does not lead to relationship and fulfillment, but rather to disappointment and even unnecessary suffering.

Its Illustration

The Roman Centurion.

A Roman soldier made a statement which prompted Jesus to say to the multitude that followed Him: "I say to you, not even in Israel have I found such great faith."[8] What was there about the Centurion's faith which produced such glowing praise from Jesus?

The Centurion was a military officer who clearly understood authority. He had a favorite servant who was very sick and about to die. There is no indication that he had ever personally seen Jesus perform any miracles. Undoubtedly, he had heard stories of how Jesus had healed the sick, and sent some Jewish friends to ask Him to come. When Jesus drew close to his home, the Centurion sent a message, "Lord, do not trouble yourself further, for I am not fit for you to come under my roof; for this reason I did not even consider myself worthy to come to you, but just say the word, and my servant will be healed."

The Centurion, humbling himself, expected Jesus to be able to heal thereby acknowledging His position of authority over disease. He interjected no conditions. Rather, he simply asked Jesus to issue the command. This unconditional faith in the person of Jesus was really a recognition of His deity, and prompted Jesus to commend him in glowing terms. The servant was healed and restored to good health.

Noah.

There was a time when God grieved that He had made humankind.[9] But one man knew and served God — and "found favor in the eyes of the Lord." Noah was to be saved from God's judgment by riding out the coming flood in an ark. It must be remembered that Noah did not live on the seaboard. He didn't even have a lakeside cabin. We can only imagine the scenario as God informed Noah of the coming deluge.

When instructed by God to build an ark, Noah probably wondered why he needed a boat where he lived. He had never needed one before. Never mind, what kind of boat should it be? God gave additional details: make it 450 feet long, 75 feet wide, and 45 feet high with three decks. Noah may have gasped, though he did have a couple spare weekends coming up. Actually, from the time of God's instructions to the time of the flood was a period of 120 years. Noah worked to build this ship for 120 years. This gives new meaning to the concept of an avocation!

But, it may be recalled, he did have three sons to help him. A study of the text, however, reveals that the first son, Shem, was born about twelve years after the command to build. I can imagine how the family got started. After eleven years of very slow progress on the ark, Noah came home discouraged. He commented to his wife that he didn't think he would ever finish building it. But, together, they hit upon a great idea — Shem. Two more good ideas quickly followed, i.e., Ham and Japheth. Now there were five who could work on the project.

It is a curiosity to wonder how Noah handled being a public spectacle in the community. This was not exactly a canoe. He couldn't hide it behind a bush. There was no escaping the fact that he was building a ship hundreds of miles from the nearest large body of water. It was probably with some regularity that the boys questioned Noah, "Dad, are you sure that you heard that message right?"

The point is that Noah's decision to build the ark was made strictly upon his acceptance of God, and, thereby the authority of His Word. For 120 years he was probably made the brunt of every joke for miles around. If I had been in his situation, I probably would have asked for a sign to keep up the faith (1/2 inch of rain per day would have been encouraging). But not Noah: "Thus Noah did; according to all that God had commanded him, so he did."

By faith Noah, being warned by God about things not yet seen, in reverence prepared an ark for the salvation of his household...and became an heir of the righteousness which is according to faith.[10]

By the time the ark was finished, it had already begun to rain. Water began to appear where it had never been before.

The fool, Noah, began to look like a genius. His formula was really quite simple — he believed God unconditionally.

The Resulting Implications

Where Am I?

At times during my quest for spiritual certainty I would end up thinking much like an agnostic. Maybe there were answers, but perhaps not. Faith is a personal thing, I thought — what works for some may not be for everyone. Reflecting upon those years from my current perspective, I believe it stemmed from the ambiguity in my thinking. I had no clear distinction between the forms of unbelief, nor did I understand genuine versus counterfeit responses to God. If I had seen my options as I do now, I think it would have given me a clearer focus and direction.

As I see it now, the first and central issue continues to be, "What position are we to take in regard to Jesus Christ?" Our response to this question alone determines whether we are in the "unbelief" or "belief" section of Figure 3.

Have I placed my faith in Jesus Christ alone for my salvation?

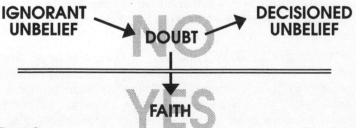

Figure 3.

Our discussion of the faith triangle in chapter four made clear the basic reasons why our response may be "no."

1. **Lack of Knowledge**: I do not know what Jesus said and did, or the reasons for faith in him.
2. **Undecided**: I have questions and emotional uncertainty about what choice to make.
3. **Willful Rejection**: I deny that Jesus needed to die for me, and I do not want to live for him.

On the other hand, to respond "yes" would mean that we agree with the apostle Peter who said that "Christ died for sins once for all, the righteous for the unrighteous, to bring you to God."[11] It also would mean that we do what the apostle Paul said that "...if you confess with your mouth, 'Jesus is Lord,' and believe in your heart that God raised him from the dead, you will be saved."[12] The apostle John tells us what will result: "...to all who received him, to those who believed in his name, he gave the right to become children of God..."[13]

But even if we say "yes," we might view this faith relationship either as a contract with conditions, or as an unconditional surrender to God.

1. **The Counterfeit: Contract "Faith"**: I give my life to God on the condition that he rewards me with health, wealth, heaven, etc. I have rights, make demands of God, and do good deeds to earn God's acceptance and special blessing.

2. **The Genuine: Surrender Faith**: I surrender my life unconditionally to God with repentance. I am accepted by his unconditional love and grace alone. I am motivated to do good deeds because of my love for him, and enabled to do so by the inner power of the Holy Spirit.

In his book, *The Screwtape Letters*, C.S. Lewis creates a series of letters from Screwtape, a professional devil and undersecretary of the department of temptation, to his nephew Wormwood, a junior tempter. Commenting on the greatest threat to the efforts of the devil in a human's life, Screwtape writes:

Do not be deceived, Wormwood, our cause is never more in danger than when a human, no longer desiring, but still intending, to do our Enemy's will, looks around upon a universe from which every trace of Him seems to have vanished, and asks why he has been forsaken, and still obeys.[14]

This is a trust that results from surrender to God because it has been persuaded by the evidence of who He is. It is not conditional on circumstances. Screwtape's description fits Jesus perfectly as He hung on the cross. He was not a victim — He chose to be there.[15] And when circumstances turned dark, He still stayed there.[16]

"It is because...the religious view of the universe [in its Christian version] seems to me to cover more of the facts of experience than any other that I have been gradually led to embrace it..."

C.E.M. Joad, *The Recovery of Belief*

What Difference Does It Make?

We have seen that the Christian faith is reasonable. The evidence for God seen through the life of Jesus is conclusive. And if it is true, we should believe in Him because of who He is, not for any benefits that may come to us. But if He is real, then His presence in our lives has to make a difference. What does He promise as a result of a faith relationship with Him?

First, if I am in right relationship with God, then I am able to realize my human potential, i.e., become all that I was intended to be in this life. After all, if I want to know how a product can best be used, I go back to the manufacturer's instructions. Likewise, if God is my creator, his specifications for my life should result in functional wholeness — intellectually, morally, and emotionally. Jesus said, "I have come that they may have life, and have it to the full."[17]

Second, if I am in right relationship with God, then I am able to realize my eternal destiny, i.e., assurance of life after death. Jesus said, "Let not your heart be troubled; believe ... in Me. In My Father's house are many dwelling places; ...I go to prepare a place for you ... I will come again, and receive you to Myself; that where I am, there you may be also."[18]

Do we dare believe that Jesus is alive, coming to earth again in the future, and will take us to live in his presence forever? The apostle Peter warned there would be scoffers who say, "Where is this 'coming' He promised? Ever since our fathers died, everything goes on as it has since the beginning of creation."[19] He then reminds his readers that the people of Noah's day scoffed in the same way. But when the flood came, Noah looked like a genius — because he believed God, and lived by His Word.

Peter adds: "By the same word the present heavens and earth are reserved for fire, being kept for the day of judgment..." Why is Jesus so slow in keeping his promise to return? "He is patient with you, not wanting anyone to perish, but everyone to come to repentance."

I remember coming to the point in my life when I realized that I no longer had any major intellectual reasons against faith in Christ. But the effect of that realization was not what I expected. Instead of being eager to take that step, I was still holding back, being cautious. What was keeping me from letting go and allowing Jesus Christ to be in control of my life? Later I came to realize what it was — something very powerful. Only God was adequate to overcome the single most important factor that kept me from faith in Jesus Christ. But when He did, I was surprised by faith.

FOCUS & DISCUSSION

1. Which of the three forms of unbelief do you think is the most common? How might your answer vary in other countries of the world?

2. Assuming you were honestly seeking personal faith in Jesus Christ, is it important to know which form of unbelief you hold? Why?

3. Is it possible to mentally misjudge a person's unbelief or faith position by the use of first impressions only? What is necessary to know for sure? What does this suggest about the importance of developing trusting relationships as a basis for discussing one's faith.

4. Sometimes we hear the expression, "seeing is believing." Read 2 Peter 3:3-10. If a person followed the expression above, when would he/she believe in the second coming of Jesus Christ? What basis do Christians have for believing in the second coming of Jesus if not according to the expression above?

SIX

WHAT IS THE BOTTOM LINE?

The Most Difficult and The Easiest Thing in the World

"The most disappointing fact in my life, I believe, is that I waited so long before I discovered the fellowship of Jesus Christ. How much more wonderful my life would have been if I had taken this step many years earlier!"
Tom Landry, Former coach of the Dallas Cowboys

"You and I have a God-shaped vacuum at the center of our being."
Blaise Pascal, 17th century French physicist

---

*S*everal years ago I served as the academic dean of a small, midwestern college. It was my job to interview candidates for positions on the faculty. I recall one candidate that was extremely likeable, but with limited ability. I enjoyed his visit to our campus immensely, but knew I had to tell him that he was not qualified for the job. After what seemed like an hour of oblique comments and nuances in my attempt to be diplomatic, the man looked at me and asked, "What's the bottom line?" In one sentence, in about five seconds, I then told him the unguarded truth.

A student that had attended one of my classes called me unexpectedly from his home during the summer break. After exchanging greetings, he talked at great length about an opportunity that was open to him. He was very complimentary to me as he went on and on. Finally, I had to ask, "What is the bottom line — why are you calling?" He then admitted that he needed $1500.

Years earlier, something similar to this had happened to me in my quest for God. I had spent many months interacting with many lines of excellent evidence. I had dialogued with several people. I weighed the pros and cons of a decision to place my faith in Jesus Christ. But the time came when I had to ask the question, "What is the spiritual bottom line?" That question made me face up to the truth that it was no longer legitimate intellectual questions that kept me from faith. I had to deal with something much more difficult — something inherent in the depths of my nature.

Identifying the Spiritual Principle

The basic principle can be identified in an incident that occurred to Peter, before he became a believer and apostle.

One day as Jesus was standing by the Lake of Gennesaret, with the people crowding around him and listening to the word of God, he saw at the water's edge two boats, left there by the fishermen, who were washing their nets. He got into one of the boats, the one belonging to Simon, and asked him to put out a little from shore. Then he sat down and taught the people from the boat.
When he had finished speaking, he said to Simon, "Put out into deep water, and let down the nets for a catch."
Simon answered, "Master, we've worked hard all night and haven't caught anything. But because you say so, I will let down the nets."
When they had done so, they caught such a large number of fish that their nets began to break. So they signaled their partners in the other boat to come and help them, and they came and filled both boats so full that they began to sink.
When Simon Peter saw this, he fell at Jesus' knees and said, "Go away from me, Lord; I am a sinful man!" For he and all his companions were astonished at the catch of fish they had taken...[1]

The Prerequisite to Faith
After fishing all night and catching nothing, Peter and his crew were washing the nets and probably eager to get some rest.

Fishing was no weekend sport for Peter, but rather his vocation. He was experienced and surely knew every feature of the lake in detail. He had undoubtedly tried every technique he knew that night. The fish just were not biting, so to speak. He was probably disgusted and not in a very good mood.

In this setting, Jesus, the carpenter and itinerant religious teacher (and novice fisherman!), suggests dropping the nets in deep water. The event that follows is most instructive. Peter is clearly reluctant because he is confident he knows exactly what will happen (and besides catching no fish, it will mean washing the nets again). To avoid embarrassment with his crew, he makes certain they know that this is not his idea ("because you say so"). Peter knows better than Jesus. This is his turf. On the beach, Peter is the "pro." Anyway, what does a traveling rabbi know about fishing. From this perspective, Peter addresses Jesus as "Master" or teacher, a title of respect but recognizing only his humanity.

Then came the astounding massive catch of fish. Peter's response is so significant. He now identifies himself as a "sinful man" and addresses Jesus as "Lord," meaning supreme in authority. The word he chose was "kurios," sometimes meaning simply "sir," but in most cases it is the translation of the Hebrew "Jehovah" or God. In view of Peter's sudden humility and response of worship, it is clear that he is attributing deity to Jesus.[2]

The spiritual principle can be seen more clearly by referring to Figure 1. The upper and lower triangles within the rectangle figuratively represent Peter and Jesus, respectively. Before the miracle catch of fish, Peter is the "pro" and imagines that he knows more than Jesus (illustrated by the base of his triangle on the left). As the incident unfolds, illustrated by the diagonal from left to right, the upper triangle representing Peter becomes smaller, and the lower triangle representing Jesus becomes larger (illustrated by the base of his triangle on the right). The miracle revealed Peter's limitations and prideful independence. The result was admission of sin and confession that Jesus was Lord. Peter's view of himself determined how he saw Jesus. This insight and brokenness is the path to a faith relationship with Jesus.

The Key to Usefulness

The illustration in Figure 1 has clear implications for our lives. Intellectually, we may be persuaded by the evidence that Jesus is the incarnation of God. But our self-sufficiency and pride may keep us from acknowledging that we need Him. As long as we perceive that we are the "pro," we will be unable to submit to Jesus' right as Lord to direct our lives. As Jesus said to the self-righteous and proud Pharisees, "It is not the healthy who need a doctor, but the sick. I have not come to call the righteous, but sinners to repentance."[3] In my own case, humbleness was not my strong suit. My pride was the greatest deterrent that had kept me from faith and dependence on Jesus. In order to follow Him in obedience I needed to experience His forgiveness and to live my life dependent on the power given to me by His Spirit.

Illustrating the Spiritual Principle

It may be helpful to illustrate how this spiritual principle was reflected in the lives of John the Baptist and Moses, two people used by God in very significant roles.

John the Baptist

John the Baptist was six months older than Jesus and had lived a life of personal denial and singleness of mind. His whole life was a preparation to announce the coming of Jesus the Messiah, "the Lamb of God who takes away the sin of the world."[4] He had many disciples and a significant popularity. He had made great sacrifices for the success he was experiencing. It was easy for me to imagine him aggressively defending his right to his position and fame.

A few months later, John's followers came to him with an understandable concern: More people were beginning to follow Jesus than John. His followers had obviously become jealous and viewed Jesus' activities as an infringement on the rights of John. But John saw it differently. He testified that "After me comes a Man who has a higher rank than I, for He existed before me ... the thong of whose sandal I am not worthy to untie."[5] In total humbleness he then declared, "A man can receive nothing, unless it has been given him from heaven ... **He must increase, but I must decrease.**"[6]

How could John do it? Because he was in a faith relationship with God and knew that doing God's eternal will was more important than temporal position and success. In other words, he had learned humility. Such an attitude was eulogized by Jesus as he later spoke of John: "I tell you, among those born of women there is no one greater than John."[7] It would have been difficult for me in my college years to imagine my competitive nature being controlled and channeled in such a humble way.

Moses

Everyone who is acquainted with the feats of Moses in Egypt would view him as a giant among men. But few realize that his reputation is based entirely on the period in his life after eighty years of age. In fact, as I will attempt to demonstrate, the operation in his earlier life of the spiritual principle identified above was the key to his greatness.

Moses was born the son of slave parents in Egypt at a time when the Pharaoh had declared a death sentence on male Hebrew newborns.[8] In a desperate move to save his life, his mother placed him in a basket in some reeds near the bank of the Nile behind the royal palace. Upon finding the crying child, Pharaoh's daughter felt pity and adopted Moses as her own son. It was by these providential circumstances that Moses enjoyed the luxury and privilege of royalty for the first forty years of his life. He is described as being "educated in all the wisdom of the Egyptians and was powerful in speech and action." Without exception, he was the most educated and powerful Jew in the world of his day.

At about the age of forty Moses committed treason by killing an Egyptian guard out of sympathy for a Hebrew slave who was being beaten. He also attempted to be an arbitrator or judge in Hebrew disputes. The significance of these activities is found in Moses' perception of himself: "...he supposed that his brethren understood that God was granting them deliverance through him."[9] There is no Biblical statement or even a hint that God had approached Moses to be His chosen deliverer at this time. God did approach him for this task forty years later — a critical delay for a very important reason.

It seems apparent that Moses had acted on his own. Why? He was the "big man" in the palace! It is clear that he overestimated his own importance and impeccability. He was above the law, a benevolent autocrat. He was the "pro." Moses' pride led him to believe that if ever there was someone who had the power to save the Hebrews from their slavery, he was that person. But he was rebuffed by his own people, and his adopted Egyptian family pronounced a death sentence upon him. He had failed, and ran for his life into the desert of modern Saudi Arabia, near the Gulf of Aqaba.

No competent vocational counselor would ever suggest a career of shepherding in the wilderness to the most educated and capable Jew in the world. Only God could know how remedial to a bad case of self-sufficiency and pride a 40-year stint in the desert would be. I can imagine how often Moses must have reflected on his failure, how badly he had "blown it." He had it all — and lost it.

Understanding Two Questions

"Who Am I?"

In this context, after forty years, God spoke to Moses from the midst of a "burning" bush in the desert, "Therefore, come now, and I will send you to Pharaoh, so that you may bring My people, the sons of Israel, out of Egypt."[10] Forty years earlier Moses might have thought, "God, I don't know you very well, but I have to hand it to you, you certainly know how to pick 'em. If anyone can do a job like that, I surely can." But at eighty years of age, after forty years in the wilderness, Moses responds, "Who am I, that I should go to Pharaoh, and that I should bring the sons of Israel out of Egypt?" This is a changed Moses, a man with humility. Besides, forty years earlier he already tried what God was asking and it didn't work. Why should it be any different now? Moses had not yet understood the significance of his own pivotal question, Who Am I?

God's response to Moses is critical to my thesis: "Certainly I will be with you ..." The implication is obvious. When Moses tried to save his people forty years earlier he had done it on his own, presumably because he thought he was quite adequate alone. That's why he failed. This time it won't be the adequacy of Moses but the power of God working through him that will guarantee success. At forty, Moses was the most educated and capable Jew in the world, a man of pride, the "pro." At eighty, he was a humbled man recognizing his need for God in order to truly succeed in his life and activities. "Who am I," or better, "who do I think I am," was the first critical question that I faced in my own spiritual bottom line. Reluctance to admit my moral failure and need was a greater deterrent to confessing faith in Jesus as Lord than any other single factor.

"God, Who Are You?"

Moses is still not sure. He has a painful memory that he has carried for forty years, that is, the rebuff of his own people: "Who made you a ruler and judge over us?" Fearing a repeat of this challenge, Moses asks, "God, who are you?" That is, what is your name, so that I can tell them who sent me. God's answer is awesome, "I Am Who I Am." Moses is to go as the instrument of God the "I Am," the One without beginning or end, the forever present tense, the Eternal One. Moses questions further: "What if they will not believe me...?"[11] God proceeded to turn his shepherd's crook into a snake and back again, and his hand leprous like snow and healed again. God was not dependent on Moses' education and capabilities. He has all the power in the universe. God had to make it clear to Moses that He was capable and desirous of filling yielded and humble human vessels with His love and power, so long as praise be properly directed to the source of all goodness, God Himself.

These are the two timeless questions that each of us has to face in mind and experience to come to faith in Jesus Christ. In spite of abilities, we must recognize that something is still missing from our lives. The paradox of power and humbleness that is evident in Moses' later life must be attractive to us. Moses was eulogized for "all the signs and wonders which the

Lord sent him to perform in the land of Egypt against Pharaoh ... and for all the mighty power and for all the great terror ... he performed." Yet Moses was described as "very humble, more than any man who was on the face of the earth."[12] It is unlikely that He learned humility in the palace in Egypt. Maybe we, too, need to learn shepherding.

Applying the Spiritual Principle

The two questions, Who Am I? and God, Who Are You?, were not formalized in my thinking at the time I was struggling with my own faith decision. But the concept was. I realized that who I thought I was did determine to a great extent how big my God could be. I had come across this idea in my reading of C.S. Lewis.

> In God you come up against something which is in every respect immeasurably superior to yourself. Unless you know God as that — and, therefore, know yourself as nothing in comparison — you do not know God at all. As long as you are proud you cannot know God.[13]

I was both hesitant and incapable of making myself smaller, so to speak. It was not until God revealed to me how big He was, that I finally saw myself small in comparison. It changed the course of my life.

"...One's relationship to God and to Jesus Christ is strictly a personal relationship...One cannot remain neutral about Him."

Charles Colson, former White House aide.

Assets and Liabilities

I was born and raised in a small farm community of southeast South Dakota. This setting was hardly the stuff from which arrogance is generated, though in jest we would express our pride that we were not from Iowa!

There were many good assets that I inherited from my parents, but two stand out as having prime importance to me.

WHAT IS THE BOTTOM LINE?

In fact, they were so important to me that I allowed them to become liabilities instead. The first asset was that I had good athletic ability. In hindsight it is apparent to me that my sphere of comparison was not very large, but from where I stood, I was "pretty good." Conference, regional and state championships in various sports gave me a basis for thinking I was better than others. This was reinforced regularly by the press I would get in our local newspaper, a weekly. Front page news was the local high school gridiron or other sports highlights. The more ink that I got, the more my ego grew. The coaches first noticed a problem when each week they had to issue me a larger helmet!

The second asset that I turned into a personal liability was intellectual acumen. High marks came easy for me, and my peers viewed me as a "brain." The recognition and awards that I got in the academic area, added to the athletic achievements, were a combined formula that fueled my self-identity and values. At that point God was unnecessary — I was doing fine without him. I wasn't so arrogant as I was self-sufficient and conceited.

It was during sophomore biology lab that I met a girl who saw life differently. Vernee, too, was very capable, but talked about a personal relationship that she had with Jesus. This was her focal point in life, determining self-acceptance and values. She also had humility. I found her attractive and we began to spend time together. Her influence set me on a spiritual search which took several years. It was also some years later that we married, and I have liked her, biology, and the Lord to whom she pointed me ever since! However, the years until then brought me to a form of bankruptcy which set me on a new course.

Restructuring and Positioning

Attending college was assumed. Sorting out the scholarship offers and holding out for the best deal was a palace experience (a la Moses), making me feel that I was in the driver's seat of my life. College years saw more athletic exploits, academic achievements, and even social recognition as king of the Valentine ball on campus.

Intellectually I was most impressed with the logical and rational, yet personable, faculty I met in the natural sciences. They were not cowed from their scientific convictions about human evolution in the face of criticism from less informed and narrow religious types. My choice of a degree in biology and secondary education contained a crusade element; that is, I would go out and save the next generation from religious narrow-mindedness to this more enlightened scientific understanding.

The height of my vanity as "the pro" came during my first year as a high school teacher of general science, biology and chemistry. I received a call from the chairman of a graduate biology program at a state university. He persuaded me to visit the university to become acquainted. But as I explained to him, the years of college with three varsity sports and a demanding science curriculum had left me tired. I wasn't looking forward immediately to graduate education. Nevertheless, I completed the application process, primarily because after teaching three months of junior high general science it was apparent to me that there were worse things than going back to school!

It was shortly after the Christmas holiday that I was called to my principal's office to receive a long-distance call. The same graduate school department chairman was calling to congratulate me on my acceptance to his biology department, and to inform me that I had been chosen as the recipient of a full-ride, national fellowship that would pay all educational expenses for a 4-5 year Ph.D. program. I am embarrassed and ashamed to recall my thoughts as I headed back to my science laboratory: "When you're good enough, this kind of thing happens to you!" I had *earned* that award. Instead of an emotion of gratefulness, it was the ultimate ego-trip. I was going to be a Ph.D!

Bankruptcy

God must have had a good laugh, so to speak, over my pretension to have the world by the tail. Shortly after arriving at the university to begin graduate studies, I met some men — Christians — who did not fit my anti-intellectual stereotype. Some were even university scientists. None of them were pushy about their faith, but did defend it with evidences that I never knew existed. Particularly, I challenged how anyone could justify belief in a Bible that propagated such prescience myths as special creation of everything by God, hell (fire and all), a real devil, and miracles — to name a few. I knew better than that!

I don't recall any adversarial relationships, but in my own heart I set out to prove that I was right. I began to read books on external evidences such as archaeology and manuscript studies. What a surprise to me that the New Testament writings were the most reliable of antiquity. Another man challenged me to read and critically study the New Testament writings firsthand. It was true that I was acquainted with the Bible since I was a child, but I had not examined its truthfulness as an adult. It seemed that for the first time in my life I was applying the tools of evidence and reason to the investigation of faith. The educational process continued for months. I was spending as much time scrutinizing the Bible and books on evidence as I was on my graduate studies in biology. Little by little it dawned on me that I was wrong about almost everything on which my skepticism was based. The interesting thing was that my reading kept bringing me back to focus on the person of Jesus. I was intrigued by him — both attracted and repelled at the same time. I liked his life — compassionate, witty, sensitive, powerful, ethical, etc. But some of his teachings were threatening — absolute authority, uncompromising holiness, and unlimited forgiveness, even toward enemies. Secretly, like Peter the fishing "pro", I still thought these were some of the things that I knew better than Jesus.

My turning point came late one night in a most unexpected way. Vernee had already gone to bed, leaving me alone to hit the books, as was my custom, into the wee hours of the morning. At some point I decided to read in the Bible for awhile. I don't recall why, but I was attracted to the Old Testament book of Job. Being competitive, I read with interest the challenge the devil presented to God concerning Job's life.[14] Reading the disaster that came to Job, I judged God as unfair and agreed with Job when he cried out that "God has wronged me."[15] I felt he was perfectly justified to say, "I will surely defend my ways to His face ... Behold now, I have prepared my case ... let me speak, and you reply."[16] I believed that God had some accounting to do.

Job got his chance. I was as surprised as Job when God appeared and spoke to him: "Who is this that darkens my counsel with words without knowledge? Brace yourself like a man; I will question you, and you shall answer me."[17] God spoke with tongue in cheek when He said he would sit at Job's feet so that He could learn from him! It is not possible to feel the full impact of this encounter without reading it in its entirety in Job 38-42. Some excerpts of God's questioning will only give the sense of it.

Where were you when I laid the earth's foundation? Tell me if you understand. Who marked off its dimensions? Surely you know!...

Have you ever given orders to the morning, or shown the dawn its place...
Have the gates of death been shown to you?...
Can you bind the beautiful Pleiades? Can you loose the cords of Orion? Can you bring forth the constellations in their seasons ...
Who endowed the heart with wisdom or gave understanding to the mind?...

It occurred to me that God was into science. This is where I was good. But these were questions that went deeper into the mysteries of origins and functions than anyone knows. However, the best was yet to come — biology.

Who provides food for the raven when its young cry out to God and wander about for lack of food? ...
Who let the wild donkey go free? Who untied his ropes?...
Do you give the horse her strength or clothe his neck with a flowing mane?...
Does the hawk take flight by your wisdom and spread his wings toward the south? Does the eagle soar at your command and build his nest on high?

After two full chapters of creation questions, God turns to Job: "Will the one who contends with the Almighty correct him? Let him who accuses God answer him!" Job's response was not what I expected: "I am unworthy — how can I reply to you? I put my hand over my mouth ..." In my conceit, I thought Job had wimped out. I did not yet see God as clearly as Job did.

God continues: "Would you discredit my justice? Would you condemn me to justify yourself? Do you have an arm like God's, and can your voice thunder like his? ...Unleash the fury of your wrath, look at every proud man and bring him low ... Then I myself will admit to you that your own right hand can save you." What follows are two more chapters of questions concerning the order and design evident in the world of science.

Suddenly, in a profoundly personal way, God was no longer talking to Job — he was talking to me! Powerfully, though not audibly, I experienced the voice of God questioning, "Don, who do you think you are anyway?" My mind's eye flashed back to the many incidents of arrogance and pride, the self-sufficiency, independence and conceit, and the strutting about like a prize rooster. In contrast I was seeing the power, wisdom and glory of the infinite God. Job's final remarks described what I was experiencing:

> I know that you can do all things; no plan of yours can be thwarted.
> You asked, "Who is this that obscures my counsel without knowledge?" Surely I spoke of things I did not understand, things too wonderful for me to know.
> You said, "Listen now, and I will speak; I will question you, and you shall answer me." My ears had heard of you but now my eyes have seen you. Therefore I despise myself and repent in dust and ashes. [18]

I slipped out of my chair to my knees and began to cry, a deep emotional thought possessing me, "Lord, I'm sorry!" I had learned that big people don't cry, that it was a sign of weakness in a man. But that night machismo didn't matter. I was devastated by my sinfulness, and I could only repeat again and again, "I'm sorry—Lord, I'm sorry." I am not certain how much time had lapsed before I was surprised by an unexpected development.

I was still on my knees reflecting on the awesomeness of God and my new desire to be under His authority. It began with the thought that I was free — of my need to win, to be number one and to prove myself; of the slavery to my ego. Oh, what a release! It was only then that I was flooded with the realization that I was forgiven. God's love through the sacrifice of Jesus, the lamb of God, had paid it all. I humbly had to admit my spiritual bankruptcy and accept forgiveness as His gift to me. Tears were flowing again, this time not of regret. They were tears of joy as my heart cried, "Thank you ... Lord, thank you ... thank you!" I was a new man — forgiven and free.

Under New Management

Many years have passed since that eventful night. I went on to complete that Ph.D. in biology, and later an M.A. in New Testament studies, but not for my ego. The reality of a personal relationship with Jesus, whom I now knew to be very much alive, created an accountability to my creator and ultimate judge. It is not as harsh as that may sound — it is the right combination of love and discipline. I have been set free to serve, and to become more myself under His Lordship than ever before —

the way I was created to be. I am at peace — under new management.

What difference has Jesus made in my life? Let me be specific.

1. I have received and continue to experience the **forgiveness of my sin**.

"He died once for the sins of all us guilty sinners, although he himself was innocent of any sin at any time, that he might bring us safely home to God."[19]

"If we confess our sins, he is faithful and just and will forgive us our sins and purify us from all unrighteousness."[20]

2. I am a **spiritual child of God** and enabled to follow Him by the Holy Spirit within me.

"Yet to all who received him, to those who believed in his name, he gave the right to become children of God..."[21]

"But the Counselor, the Holy Spirit, whom the Father will send in my name, will teach you all things and will remind you of everything I have said to you."[22]

3. I am at **peace with God** and do not fear judgment.

"For God did not send the Son into the world to judge the world; but that the world should be saved through Him. He who believes in Him is not judged..."[23]

4. I have the **assurance of eternal life** after death.

"I am the resurrection and the life; he who believes in Me shall live even if he dies..."[24]

"These things I have written to you who believe in the name of the Son of God, in order that you may know that you have eternal life."[25]

It must be understood that I claim none of these because I consider myself worthy, or have done some deed to earn them. The Bible says that "Because of his kindness you have been saved through trusting Christ. And even trusting is not of yourselves; it too is a gift from God. Salvation is not a reward for the good we have done, so none of us can take any credit for it." My wife, Vernee, and I both recognize that we would not have stayed together these thirty years if not for the grace to forgive and change — which comes from Him. Our two sons have come to acknowledge Jesus as Savior and Lord. What hope there is in knowing that when our family relationship here must end, death will only serve to reunite us once again, this time for all eternity. Every aspect of my life has been enriched under the new management of Jesus Christ.

Following Jesus Christ has been an experience of increasing challenge, adventure and happiness. He is totally worthwhile. How true are His words: 'I am come that they might have life, and that they might have it more abundantly.'"
                    Mark Hatfield, Senator from Oregon

A Personal Invitation

Clark Pinnock has expressed in a succinct way what I have personally discovered about faith in my life journey.

I am convinced that faith needs to face up to the truth question and that the Christian message fits the facts. It is not a presupposition that has to be accepted on authority or a self-evident truth that needs no argument; it is a solid truth claim that can be tested and verified across the whole range of human experience. It meets our existential needs, makes sense out of our religious intuitions, stands up under rational scrutiny, corresponds with the historical evidence and speaks to today's moral necessities...
To stand beneath the lordship of Christ is not a misfortune or humiliation for you. It is rather the entrance into abundant life and an existence that is truly desirable.
Therefore, I make this appeal to you: open yourself up to God, confess your failure to live a just and holy life, and determine to follow the Lord Jesus. Act upon the evidence that stands before you and accept the saving offer that is being extended.[26]

Jesus respects your will. He waits for an invitation — a decision on your part to ask him to forgive and take the wheel. No one can say it better than He did.

Come to me, all you who are weary and burdened, and I will give you rest. Take my yoke upon you and learn from me, for I am gentle and humble in heart, and you will find rest for your souls. For my yoke is easy and my burden is light.[27]

His promises do not mean much until you reach out and take them for yourself. If you are ready to move into a relationship with God through faith in Jesus Christ, tell him so through prayer. This simple prayer may be used if you are not sure what to say:

Dear God, I want to know the reality of a personal relationship with you. I acknowledge that my sin has separated me from you. I repent, and accept Jesus Christ as my Savior because He died in my place. Please give me the gift of the Holy Spirit to direct my life, and enable me to understand and follow your Word from this day on. Thank you for making me your spiritual child and giving me the assurance of eternal life. Amen.

FOCUS & DISCUSSION

1. It is stated in the text that a refusal to admit one's own identity as a sinner is a greater deterrent to recognizing Jesus' deity than any other single factor. What is meant by this?
2. What two questions must each person ask and honestly answer along the path to faith? Why is self-righteous pride such a powerful force in our lives?
3. What is the "bottom line" in a person's getting right with God? Why is it a difficult thing to deal with? Is the difficulty primarily intellectual in nature?
4. In what sense is faith in Jesus Christ very easy?
5. What does the fact that salvation is a gift imply about a Christian's basis for assurance of eternal life? What is it dependent upon?

ANOTHER STEP

I am interested in getting to know you and assisting you spiritually in any way that I can. Particularly, if after reading this book, you have decided to receive Jesus Christ as your Savior and Lord, I invite you to call or write to indicate your decision. In response, I will send free literature that has been designed for your spiritual growth. A life of faith will enable you to trust God increasingly with every detail of your life. The Bible says,

"And now just as you trusted Christ to save you, trust him, too, for each day's problems; ...See that you go on growing in the Lord, and become strong and vigorous..." Colossians 2:6-7

I look forward to hearing from you as you take this additional step in your relationship and walk with Him.

On the other hand, you may have read this book and still have questions. Indeed, you may have objections or an evaluation concerning the contents. In any case, I would appreciate hearing from you. As appropriate, I would be happy to talk with you, send an annotated apologetic reading guide, or share materials that may be helpful. The subject of Jesus Christ is important enough to justify taking another step to resolve whatever questions may remain. I look forward to hearing from you.

For comments or further help, call or write:

Dr. Don Bierle
Faith Studies International
P.O. Box 103
Chaska, MN 55318
612/361-0850
800/964-1447

NOTES

Chapter One: What Are We Here For?

1. Clark Pinnock, *A Case for Faith* (Minneapolis: Bethany, 1980), p. 24.
2. Michael Cassidy, *Christianity for the Open-Minded* (Downers Grove: InterVarsity, 1978), p. 12.
3. An ecologist would suggest that it finds meaning in returning to the soil in a natural cycle of nutrients. But this requires death, the sacrifice of the individual, for some undemonstrated higher cause.
4. Pinnock, *A Case for Faith*, p. 34.
5. Paul Little, *Know Why You Believe* (Downers Grove: InterVarsity, 1988), p. 15.
6. Francis A. Schaeffer, *The Complete Works of Francis A. Schaeffer: A Christian Worldview*, vol. 1: A Christian View of Philosophy and Culture (Westchester, Illinois: Crossway Books, 1982), pp. 101ff.

Chapter Two: Can I Believe The Bible?

1. For this evidence, see F.F. Bruce, *Jesus and Christian Origins Outside the New Testament* (Grand Rapids: William B. Eerdmans, 1974); and Gary R. Habermas, *Ancient Evidence for the Life of Jesus* (Nashville: Thomas Nelson, 1984).
2. Taken from her regular column in the Star and Tribune newspaper of Minneapolis/St. Paul. Date unknown.
3. Gaius Julius Caesar, *Caesar's War Commentaries*, edited and translated by John Warrington (New York: E.P. Dutton & Co., 1958).
4. F.F. Bruce, *The Books and the Parchments* (Westwood, N.J.: Fleming H. Revell, 1963), p. 178.
5. Frederic Kenyon, *Our Bible and the Ancient Manuscripts* (New York: Harper & Brothers, 1941), p. 23.
6. Frederic Kenyon, *The Bible and Modern Scholarship* (London: John Murray, 1948), p. 20.
7. F.F. Bruce, *The New Testament Documents: Are They Reliable?* (Downers Grove: InterVarsity, 1960), p. 15.
8. Bruce M. Metzger, *Chapters in the History of New Testament Textual Criticism* (Grand Rapids: Eerdmans, 1963), cited by Geisler and Nix, *A General Introduction to the Bible* Chicago: Moody, 1968), pp. 366f.
9. Bruce, *The New Testament Documents*, pp. 19-20.
10. Kenyon, *Our Bible and the Ancient Manuscripts*, p. 23.
11. Frederic Kenyon, *The Bible and Archaeology* (New York: Harper & Row, 1940), pp. 288f.

12. Luke 3:1-2a
13. Bruce, *The New Testament Documents*, p. 82.
14. Acts 17:6
15. Bruce, *The New Testament Documents*, p. 82.
16. John 19:32-33
17. Vassilios Tzaferis, "Crucifixion—The Archaeological Evidence," *Biblical Archaeology Review* 9 (Jan/Feb 1985):44-53.
18. See both Paul L. Maier, *First Christmas* (San Francisco: Harper & Row, 1971), pp. 15-22; and Gary Habermas, *Ancient Evidence for the Life of Jesus* (Nashville: Thomas Nelson, 1984), pp. 152-53.
19. Robert Bull, "Caesarea Maritima — The Search for Herod's City," *Biblical Archaeology Review* 8 (May/June 1982):24-41.
20. A.N. Sherwin-White, *Roman Society and Roman Law in the New Testament*, (Oxford: Clarendon Press, 1963) cited in Clark Pinnock, *A Case for Faith* (Minneapolis: Bethany, 1980), p. 77.
21. Bruce, *The New Testament Documents*, p. 88.
22. Genesis 19
23. Clifford Wilson, *Ebla Tablets: Secrets of a Forgotten City* (San Diego: Master Books, 1979), pp. 36-37.
24. Aharon Kempinski, "Hittites in the Bible — What Does Archeology Say?" *Biblical Archaeology Review* 5 (Sept/Oct 1979): 20-44.
25. W.F. Albright, *The Archaeology of Palestine*, Rev. Ed. (Harmondsworth, Middlesex: Pelican Books, 1960), pp. 127f.
26. Millar Burrows, *What Mean These Stones?* (New York: Meridian Books, 1956), p. 1.
27. Nelson Glueck, *Rivers in the Desert* (Philadelphia: Jewish Publications Soc. of America, 1969), p. 31.
28. Kenyon, *The Bible and Archaeology*, p. 279.
29. K.A. Kitchen, *The Bible in its World* (Downers Grove: InterVarsity, 1977), p. 132.
30. Acts 2:22, 32
31. Acts 2:41
32. Acts 26:26
33. Bruce, *The New Testament Documents*, p. 46.
34. Julius Muller's critique of D.F. Strauss' theory that the gospel accounts are mere legends has never been answered: "Most decidedly must a considerable interval of time be required for such a complete transformation of a whole history by popular tradition, when the series of legends are formed in the same territory where the heroes actually lived and wrought. Here one cannot imagine how such a series of legends could arise in an historical age, obtain universal respect, and supplant the historical recollection of the true character and connecting of their heroes' lives in the

minds of the community, if eyewitnesses were still at hand, who could be questioned respecting the truth of the recorded marvels. Hence, legendary fiction, as it likes not the clear present time, but prefers the mysterious gloom of grey antiquity, is wont to seek a remoteness of age, along with that of space, and to remove its boldest and more rare and wonderful creations into a very remote and unknown land." Julius Muller, *The Theory of Myths, in its Application to the Gospel History, Examined and Confuted* (London: John Chapman, 1844), p. 26; in William Craig, *The Son Rises* (Chicago: Moody Press, 1981), p. 101.

35. Norman Geisler and William Nix, *A General Introduction to the Bible* (Chicago: Moody, 1968), p. 124.
36. C.S. Lewis, *Surprised by Joy* (London: Collins, 1955), pp. 178f, 182, 187f.
37. Frank Morison, *Who Moved the Stone* (Grand Rapids: Zondervan, 1977 reprint), pp. 8-12.

Chapter Three: Is Jesus Really God?

1. See Luke 4:14-30
2. Isaiah 61:1-2
3. But Jesus' claim to be the Messiah probably was intended as a claim to be God as well. Jesus quoted that day from Isaiah 61:1-2. According to the same Old Testament book (9:6), the Messiah was called, "Mighty God, Eternal Father." Thus, Jesus' claim was equivalent to saying, "I'm God."
4. John 4:25-26; Mark 8:27-30
5. See Matthew 22:41-46
6. See John 8:53-59
7. See Exodus 3:14
8. See John 10:22-33
9. See John 8:23-24
10. See John 5:21; 10:27-28; 11:25-26
11. See Matthew 28:18 and John 19:7
12. John 19:7
13. John W. Montgomery, *History and Christianity* (Minneapolis: Bethany, 1965), p. 63.
14. See Luke 5:17-26
15. Luke 5:24-26
16. John 9:1ff
17. See Luke 13:1-5
18. See Luke 7:11-16
19. See Luke 8:22-25

20. Matthew 7:28
21. John 10:37,38
22. See Luke 4:1-13; Matthew 14:33; 28:17; and John 9:38
23. Compare Matthew 21:15-16 with Psalm 8:2
24. See Luke 4:33-36 and Matthew 12:24
25. See John 8:46; 14:6; and Mark 10:45 with Psalm 49:7-9
26. Luke 9:20
27. Jon A. Buell and O. Quentin Hyder, *Jesus: God, Ghost or Guru?* (Grand Rapids: Zondervan, 1978), p. 102.
28. For example, see Matthew 16:21; 17:9; 26:32
29. John 2:19
30. Michael Green, *Man Alive* (Downers Grove: InterVarsity, 1968), pp. 53-54, as quoted in Josh McDowell, *Evidence that Demands a Verdict* (San Bernardino: Here's Life Publishers, 1972), p. 201.
31. See Luke 24:11 and John 20:24ff
32. Matthew 28:12, 13, 15
33. Paul L. Maier, *First Easter* (San Francisco: Harper and Row, 1973), p.120.
34. 1 Corinthians 15:5,6
35. C.H. Dodd, "The Appearances of the Risen Christ: A study in the form criticism of the Gospels," in *More New Testament Studies* (Manchester: U. of Manchester Press, 1968), p. 128.
36. For the Apostle Paul's own testimony see Acts 9:1-22.
37. See Matthew 26:56, 69-75; John 20:19
38. Gary Habermas, *The Resurrection of Jesus* (New York: University Press of America, 1984), p. 39.
39. J.N.D. Anderson, *The Evidence for the Resurrection* (Downers Grove: InterVarsity, 1966), pp. 3f.
40. C.S. Lewis, *Mere Christianity* (New York: Macmillan, 1952), pp. 55-56.

Chapter Four: Can Faith Be Reasonable?

1. Romans 10:13-17
2. Romans 10:17 (The New Testament in Modern English, J.B. Phillips)
3. See 1 Corinthians 15:12-19
4. Romans 10:16-21
5. Matthew 21:28-32
6. James 2:14-26
7. Luke 6:46-49
8. See Genesis 15:1-6 and 22:1-19 for this discussion of Abraham
9. Hebrews 11:17-19

10. For evidence concerning this identification, see 2 Chronicles 3:1; 1 Chronicles 21:15-30; Book of Jubilees 18:13; Josephus (Antiquities I. xii. 1; VII. xiii. 4).
11. John 1:29
12. Galatians 3:6-9
13. See Romans 4:16-25
14. John 7:37-39
15. John 14:15-17, 23
16. 1 Corinthians 6:19
17. Ephesians 1:13-14
18. John 3:1-18
19. Mark 7:20-23
20. Ephesians 2:8-9
21. John 6:44
22. Titus 3:3-7
23. Philippians 2:13
24. 1 John 5:11-13
25. John 3:16 and Romans 6:23
26. Josh McDowell, *Evidence that Demands a Verdict* (San Bernardino: Here's Life, 1979), p. 327f.
27. John 14:1-3
28. See John 5:21-29 and 12:48
29. Romans 8:1-2

Chapter Five: Where Am I?

1. Elizabeth Elliot, *Through Gates of Splendor* (New York: Harper and Brothers, 1957).
2. Ephesians 4:18
3. 1 Timothy 1:13
4. For examples see Matthew 16:21; Mark 9:31; 10:32-34; John 2:19-22.
5. John 20:24-29
6. See Numbers 13 and 14
7. Numbers 14:11
8. See Luke 7:2-10
9. This discussion of Noah is based on the text in Genesis 6-8.
10. Hebrews 11:7
11. 1 Peter 3:18
12. Romans 10:9
13. John 1:12
14. C.S. Lewis, *The Screwtape Letters* (Chicago: Lord and King Associates, 1976), p. 51.

15. See John 10:17-18; Mark 10:45; and Matthew 26:53
16. See Matthew 26:47-56 and 27:38-54
17. John 10:10
18. John 14:1-3
19. See 2 Peter 3:3-13

Chapter Six: What Is The Bottom Line?

1. Luke 5:1-9
2. A similar response using the same word "kurios" is given by Thomas in John 20:28.
3. Luke 5:31-32
4. For background on John the Baptist see Mark 1:1-8; 6:14-32; Luke 1:13-17; 3:1-20.
5. John 1:26-30
6. John 3:26-30
7. Luke 7:28
8. For the Biblical accounts of Moses' life see Exodus 2 and 3, and Acts 7:17-38.
9. Acts 7:25
10. See Exodus 3:10ff for this historical event.
11. See Exodus 4:1ff
12. See Deuteronomy 34:10-12 and Numbers 12:3 for this paradox.
13. C.S. Lewis, *Mere Christianity*, (New York: The Macmillan Company, 1952), p. 111.
14. See Job 1 and 2
15. Job 19:6-7
16. Job 13:15-22
17. Job 38:2-3
18. Job 42:2-6
19. 1 Peter 3:18
20. 1 John 1:9
21. John 1:12
22. John 14:26
23. John 3:17-18
24. John 11:25
25. 1 John 5:13
26. Clark Pinnock, *A Case for Faith*, (Minneapolis: Bethany, 1980), pp. 119, 121-2.
27. Matthew 11:28-30

Step 1 God's Purpose: Peace and Life

God loves you and wants you to experience peace and life—abundant and eternal.

The Bible Says . . .

". . . we have peace with God through our Lord Jesus Christ." Romans 5:1

"For God so loved the world that He gave His only begotten Son, that whoever believes in Him should not perish but have everlasting life." John 3:16

". . . I have come that they may have life, and that they may have it more abundantly." John 10:10b

Since God planned for us to have peace and the abundant life right now, why are most people not having this experience?

Step 2 Our Problem: Separation

God created us in His own image to have an abundant life. He did not make us as robots to automatically love and obey Him, but gave us a will and a freedom of choice.

We chose to disobey God and go our own willful way. We still make this choice today. This results in separation from God.

The Bible Says . . .

"For all have sinned and fall short of the glory of God." Romans 3:23

"For the wages of sin is death, but the gift of God is eternal life in Christ Jesus our Lord." Romans 6:23

Our choice results in separation from God.

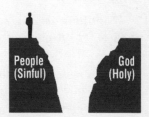

People (Sinful) God (Holy)

Our Attempts

There is only one remedy for this problem of separation.

Through the ages, individuals have tried in many ways to bridge this gap . . . without success . . .

The Bible Says . . .

"There is a way that seems right to man, but in the end it leads to death." Proverbs 14:12

"But your iniquities have separated you from God; and your sins have hidden His face from you, so that He will not hear." Isaiah 59:2

Step 3 God's Remedy: The Cross

Jesus Christ is the only answer to this problem. He died on the Cross and rose from the grave, paying the penalty for our sin and bridging the gap between God and people.

The Bible Says . . .

". . . God is on one side and all the people on the other side, and Christ Jesus, Himself man, is between them to bring them together . . ."
1 Timothy 2:5

"For Christ also has suffered once for sins, the just for the unjust, that He might bring us to God . . ." 1 Peter 3:18a

"But God demonstrates His own love for us in this: While we were still sinners, Christ died for us." Romans 5:8

God has provided the only way . . . we must make the choice . . .

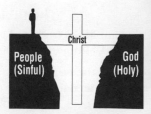

Step 4 Our Response: Receive Christ

We must trust Jesus Christ and receive Him by personal invitation.

The Bible Says . . .

"Behold, I stand at the door and knock. If anyone hears My voice and opens the door, I will come in to him and dine with him, and he with Me." Revelation 3:20

"But as many as received Him, to them He gave the right to become children of God, even to those who believe in His name." John 1:12

". . . if you confess with your mouth the Lord Jesus and believe in your heart that God has raised Him from the dead, you will be saved." Romans 10:9

Are you here . . . or here?

People — Sin, Rebellion, Separation

Christ

God — Peace, Forgiveness, Abundant Life, Eternal Life

Is there any good reason why you cannot receive Jesus Christ right now?

How to receive Christ:

1. Admit your need (I am a sinner).
2. Be willing to turn from your sins (repent).
3. Believe that Jesus Christ died for you on the Cross and rose from the grave.
4. Through prayer, invite Jesus Christ to come in and control your life through the Holy Spirit. (Receive Him as Lord and Savior.)

What to Pray:

Dear Lord Jesus,

   I know that I am a sinner and need Your forgiveness. I believe that You died for my sins. I want to turn from my sins. I now invite You to come into my heart and life. I want to trust and follow You as Lord and Savior.

In Jesus' name. Amen.

_____   _____
Date   Signature

God's Assurance: His Word

If you prayed this prayer,
The Bible Says...

**"For 'whoever calls upon the name of the Lord will be saved.'"
Romans 10:13**

Did you sincerely ask Jesus Christ to come into your life? Where is He right now? What has He given you?

"For it is by grace you have been saved, through faith—and this is not from yourselves, it is the gift of God—not by works, so that no one can boast." Ephesians 2:8,9

The Bible Says...

**"He who has the Son has life; he who does not have the Son of God does not have life. These things I have written to you who believe in the name of the Son of God, that you may know that you have eternal life, and that you may continue to believe in the name of the Son of God."
1 John 5:12–13, NKJV**

Receiving Christ, we are born into God's family through the supernatural work of the Holy Spirit who indwells every believer...this is called regeneration or the "new birth."

This is just the beginning of a wonderful new life in Christ. To deepen this relationship you should:

1. Read your Bible every day to know Christ better.
2. Talk to God in prayer every day.
3. Tell others about Christ.
4. Worship, fellowship, and serve with other Christians in a church where Christ is preached.
5. As Christ's representative in a needy world, demonstrate your new life by your love and concern for others.

God bless you as you do.

Billy Graham

If you want further help in the decision you have made, write to:
Billy Graham Evangelistic Association P.O. Box 779, Minneapolis, Minnesota 55440-0779